The Old Soul's Guide

A Handbook for a Joyous Existence

Anamika®

Compiled and edited by
Carolyn Hawkins

Mountain Cat Productions • Santa Barbara, CA

The Old Soul's Guide
A Handbook for a Joyous Existence

by Anamika®

Compiled and Edited by Carolyn Hawkins

Published by:
Mountain Cat Productions
255 Elise Place #A
Santa Barbara, CA 93109 USA
(805)568-0909
MounatainCatProductions.com

Cover Design by Lynda Rae

ISBN, print ed. 0-9755546-0-3
First Printing 2004

Library of Congress Cataloging-in-Publication Data
Anamika®, The Old Soul's Guide: A Handbook for a Joyous Existence/ - 1st ed.
2004108711

TABLE OF CONTENTS

ABOUT ANAMIKA®

Anamika is a spiritual teacher, author and international workshop leader. She transmits the energies of Sakkara Temple of Awakening®, blending her gifts of energy transmission, clairvoyance, clairaudience, clairsentience, and telepathy with her background in music, movement, dance, psychology and healing.

The energy transmissions of Sakkara Temple of Awakening® provide an infusion of Divine Love, catalyzing a shift in consciousness for personal and collective awakening. Sakkara is a portal into the Infinite so that we may come into a more direct experience of our own God consciousness. The experience of Sakkara Temple of Awakening® is offered in workshops, intensives and online.

Having completed her undergraduate degree at Wellesley College, Anamika went on to nontraditional education in which she received an M.A in Psychology from Beacon College, a Ph.D. in Psychology from Columbia Pacific University and graduated from the Barbara Brennan School of Healing. She has appeared on numerous radio and television shows, including *The Oprah Winfrey Show.*

Anamika's personal odyssey of spiritual awakening as well as the stages of development in the journey of the soul are chronicled in her forthcoming books. She shares her home in Malibu, California with her cream and gold Afghan Hounds, Shaqqara and Shalim.

INTRODUCTION

There is a journey that all souls make. It is a journey from not even knowing you exist to total consciousness that you exist in an interplay with all the higher eternal forces. In order to join these forces that know themselves as eternal, you must embrace the truth that you are eternal on every level of your being.

A soul does not even know it exists until it recognizes itself as existing, but must first create some sense of identity to know of its existence. You are then asked to discreate the identity that you have created, giving it up to find a truer sense of self.

Spiritual guidance for the journey comes from within and is provided to you if you devotedly and persistently seek it. In seeking, truth beyond your present understanding must be embraced. If you are willing to embrace truth, you will have to become honest with yourself, facing the terror of your own mortality, struggles and beliefs. This creates an openness in you that is attractive, indeed compelling to the Truth of This Existence, who falls in love with you for your openness.

A soul goes through much on this journey and by the time you have been around for a while and are an old soul, you will find that happiness is quite different for you than for the younger soul. It is very difficult for you, as an old soul, to be happy because you have done many things before in many lifetimes: romance, money, power, etc. You can appreciate those things, but it is very hard for old souls to be happy in those ways. Your conditioning though, will still drive you to find fulfillment in these ways. This can cause you to become more and more despairing because you may not feel the hole in your soul being addressed.

Now being an old soul, you have merged many times into the experience of the Creator and will often confuse yourself with God. You may even feel that your power is infinite, so when you draw upon what you feel should be an infinite store, you will still lack and may feel as though your God has failed you. This is a devastating dilemma for the old soul.

In fact you are not God, rather the doorway to the Infinite lies deep within you. You must go within yourself to the doorway and call upon the Infinite to help you. The Infinite will fill you with what you need, then you can meet with what you must do. In this way, as an old soul, you become dependent on an infinite store rather than a magnificent but finite self. This is part of the psychic change, a shift into a dependency upon the Infinite from the dependency upon the beautiful but finite self.

Another peculiarity of being an old soul is that you have learned from your many life experiences that very few people outside of you will take care of you, so you seek total and absolute self-sufficiency. You seek freedom from dependencies, which means you focus on everything like self-realization, self-fulfillment, self-this and self-that until you are completely self-ish. You cannot find freedom from your own obsessive thoughts of yourself.

The solution for an old soul is selflessness, but that is the last thing you will ever seek. You will remember lifetimes of trying to do that in which you were abused and exploited. Thus, selflessness seems like the last thing that would help. Therefore, you, the old soul, must have a psychic change, a transformation in understanding of who and what you are that comes from seeking the spiritual experience. You must seek and cultivate a conscious contact with the Source of Existence, and then carry the message that you are transformed by the Creator and not by your desire to perfect yourself. This is called service.

The desire to perfect yourself creates pain, the pain of purging yourself instead of accepting yourself. While in words it sounds so simple to just accept yourself, in life experience it is harder because it is an experience, not a philosophy, dogma, teaching, discipline or religion. It is a spiritual experience.

The Creator gives many gifts along the way that come from outside the old soul's personal control. This is enormously frustrating because you are master controllers. When you see gifts from the Supreme coming, you appreciate them, but will also usually try to think of ways you can get more or make certain this always happens. The Creator sort of blessedly takes you and plays with you, giving you love in a thousand forms to replace your thousand forms of fear.

As an old soul, do not be surprised when you see the thousand forms of fear, which are slowly replaced by a thousand forms of grace. This is a gradual process that is brought by life experience. Your life journey increasingly transmutes an old way of thinking into a newer way of thinking and being with which you become utterly identified. As a result of your spiritual experience and service, a self is revealed to you that you did not know, but had always sensed yourself to be.

You will seemingly rocket into the fourth dimension of existence where you will feel unquestionably a bit insane. There is no doubt about it. You will not feel that much in control, but you will feel increasingly protected and serene. You will join with a family of others who feel precisely the same way and who will support you until you complete with this world.

— *Sun Bear*

The Old Soul's Guide is a compilation of gems of wisdom inspired by the Ascended Masters in spirit. These Spirit Guides began speaking with me in 1989 through my dear friend Mataare, who is an extraordinary trance channel. The Guides provided penetrating insight with infinite patience, exquisite tenderness, humbling confrontation and gentle humor. They helped unravel and transmute my perceptions about myself, life, spirituality and God.

The teachings of the Guides and their life stories shed light on the process of completing our soul's business and transition into a new dimension of being, thus embracing the radiance of our soul's infinite nature. They refer to this transfiguration as awakening or ascension.

I share their gems of wisdom so that you might enjoy the exquisite pleasure of enhancing your own personal relationship with the Spirit Guides as well as receive helpful insight for your own awakening.

These excerpts are inspired by the teachings of the Guides and are presented alphabetically by topic. At the end of each piece you will find the name of the Guide who inspired it. When several Guides are credited as the inspiration of a piece, they were speaking as a blended consciousness through the first one noted. May these words bring a light of deeper understanding to the magnificent journey of your own soul.

Anamika

The Guides

Amatunkwa: very large Native American Guide who serves as a protector

Astarte: from the Goddess lineage

Balthazar: teacher of Yeshua (the man later called Jesus)

Cassandra: from the Goddess lineage

Chief Great White Eagle (Chief): a Native American Chief and an incarnation of John the Beloved.

Constance: a Seraph and Herald

Devorah: Queen of the Gypsies

Dormor: nickname for Bodhidarma, the Chinese Buddha

Dr. Tsong: Chinese herbalist and acupuncturist

Enoch: Lord of Light

Francesco: St. Francis of Assisi, Italian Saint

God: the name of God is God. The name is not a title. The name of God is a vibration, an ineffable name that is a living presence, that is remembrance.

Imhotep: Egyptian architect

Ishtara: from the Goddess lineage

Isis: from the Goddess lineage, Egyptian Queen, married to Osiris

Kira: Indian Guide

Lao Tzu: Chinese sage

Merlin: the title of the man named Ambrosius Merlinius, THE Merlin.

Milarepa: Tibetan Master

Miriam: Mother of Yeshua (the man later called Jesus)

Motambi Motombi (Mo): African Chief

Morgana: High Priestess of Avalon during times of King Arthur

Nemo: Devorah's panther

Olga and Helga: Rumanian sisters and seers

Philos: Keeper of the Akashic Records, never been incarnate in human form.

Quan Yin: Divine Mother aspect

Red Sky: Native American Guide, a heyeohkah (trickster)

Ribazar Tarz: an eight hundred year old Tibetan Shaman Master who is still living.

Jhenrhett Turonok: a prior Atlantian incarnation of Merlin

Sam Strong Body: Native American Guide

Shiva: destroyer aspect of the Triple Goddess

Shakyamuni Siddhartha Guatama: the Buddha

Sky Walker: Native American Guide

Sun Bear: group soul of Native American Shamans. The man named Sun Bear, who died several years ago, has merged with the group soul.

Tall Trees: Native American Guide

Two Trees: Native American Guide

Yeshua: ancient Hebrew name of the man the Romans later called Jesus

ACCEPTANCE

Acceptance only seems to happen in people when they have nothing left anymore.

– *Chief Great White Eagle*

❖❖❖

There are a few basic principles or cosmic laws about how all of life works. If these are accepted, then life works better, but very few people do this well, and nobody does it perfectly. One of these principles is, "Wherever you go, there you are," which means acceptance.

– *Sun Bear, Chief Great White Eagle, Tall Trees, Two Trees, Sky Walker, Sam Strong Body, Red Sky*

❖❖❖

Acceptance simply means that there is a decision from which there is no return, no other possibility. The decision is that absolutely nothing matters, not even God realization, because there is a totality of peace. In other words, there is a complete understanding on every level that you are totally taken care of by the universe and that all things are as they ought to be. Nothing needs to be different from the way that it is. There is total appreciation and acceptance, no destiny, no projection, nothing more that you want to happen other than what is happening right now. No desire of any kind exists for anything other than what is. There is no future, no 'yet to be'. Everything is in its perfect state right now.

This complete and total acceptance allows you to go onward into the next dimension. Acceptance is total appreciation of everything that you are right now and appreciation of everything that is around you, including all circumstances and conditions, in all their manifestation. This is a state of being, not simply an intellectual concept.

– *Philos*

❖❖❖

Acceptance is a feeling place for the spirit, not the mind, where you know that you are one with the will of God. Your mind will never understand and will always question what your heart and spirit know. You cannot see that you have done the will of the Creator by looking for evidence that helps your mind understand. Rather, your heart simply accepts because you have meditated, prayed, asked, thanked and repeated all of that every day. Your heart then feels good and you are serene about faith for today. You feel that you have done your best for today and your spirit says, "For today I have done it and that is all that I can do."

This acceptance will not be met with any kind of intellectual or mental understanding, but will be a total embrace, which can never be let go of or interfered with because no one can take it from you. The only thing that will happen is that you will grow firm in acceptance and you will never doubt it, then your strength will light the fire of others. On this you can rely.

– Chief Great White Eagle, Sun Bear, Miriam

❖❖❖

Is it really lowering your standard to accept yourself where you are and others where they are, or is that what it means to become a higher being?

– Merlin, Chief Great While Eagle, Amatunkwa and Enoch

❖❖❖

Acceptance takes place in an environment of love. If there is not love for self and perhaps for others as well, then you cannot accept in totality what you are right now. The tendency will be to reject some part of who you are right now, or some part of your experience right now. One way of rejecting it is, "Am I making this up? Is this real? What is going on?" These are all manifestations of resistance.

When you sense your own resistance that is good. Do not fight with your own resistance, just accept it too. When you feel resistance, acknowledge, "Oh, this must be a part of the resistance." Be present with it and go right into it. It is very easy to go into resistance because it means simply letting go to whatever is going on. That is what self-love is all about, letting go to what is going on even though you might appear to be very silly. I have been called a good deal more than silly in my time!

– Merlin

AGENTS OF THE LIGHT

It is the Creator's mission to inject light and life into every dimension and world in existence where there are agents through which to work. Agents are continually presenting themselves and the Creator responds. Yet the people of this world, because they have not yet reached a high level of awakening, are continually taking their lives back after they have offered them to the Creator. They then do not serve any further to bring in the light as is needed. When this occurs the world continues to be dominated by something other than love because the light can only come when there are those who are willing.

– *Philos*

❖❖❖

Indeed the world is increasingly shifting, for much is pouring into the world through the agents of the light. Each person plays an important role so that others who are willing may embrace the light. The agents of the light are afforded a beauty and an incredible opportunity for they are surrounded by energy, grace, and light. Their existence is indeed blessed.

– *Yeshua*

AKASHIC RECORD

Akasha is a record of all that ever was and ever shall be in this universe: all that is now, all that exists now as potential, all that may have been, and all which might be, as well as all parallel existences to this one. Those who have touched upon parallel existences might think that there are infinite existences in that they reflect a possibility of choices that may seem infinite. They however are not infinite, but are numbered.

It is not desire alone that will allow you to view Akasha and thereby come to a sense of what shall be or what is right for you. It is not your need that declares and determines what it is that will allow you to see what is available. It is not psychic skills and aptitudes that define what you are able to understand of what is within the record. While all of those things are factors, they are not the determining factor. What determines it is the refinement of your conscious contact with the Source of Existence. It is your willingness to allow the Source of Existence Itself to enter into your conscious understanding that creates a change sufficient for you to be able to access the truth of this existence as relates to you.

If you are not willing to allow the Source to come into your being and create the necessary changes, to that extent you must have other kinds of lessons here in this world to come to the wisdom of allowing that. As you open, the Akashic record is opened in any number of ways such as through past life regressions, hypnosis and many other forms of journeying. But, you shall not be able to view or experience what you wish according to your desire, sincerity, aspiration or inspiration alone. You must be willing at some point to allow the Source Power Itself, the Creator of All, to enmesh Itself with your being and cause you to become as It would have you be. Ultimately, total and absolute surrender is the path.

How much are you willing to allow that enmeshment? How much are you willing to surrender consciously into It, allowing It to change what you think is important and your aspirations and goals? How much are you fixed upon what you believe is absolutely right for you because you are seeking to bring about a manifestation of some conjuring of your imagination?

The time eventually must come whereby you, the seeker of truth, must begin to say to the Spirit of the Universe, "What would you have of me?" At some juncture this must be done, and whatsoever you must do to arrive at such a juncture is the path.

– Philos

ALLOWING

People are so busy trying to strangle the world into bringing them what they want that they cannot understand the grace of allowing and the freedom it brings. When you grow in harmony with the universe, you let it give and take what it wishes. This does not mean you cannot get what you want, but that you then get what you want when it helps you grow and helps you do what you are here to do. Otherwise, you get what you truly most need.

– Chief Great White Eagle, Olga and Helga

ALTRUISTIC PLANE

The altruistic plane is accessed by increasingly becoming concerned with the welfare of others, specifically by seeking to carry the message of the light, which has been revealed through your conscious contacts with that light. This means you carry spiritual awakening into the world and then the Creator of All shall resolve your problems. These problems, which can be serious ones, can only be addressed on a spiritual and altruistic plane.

– *Yeshua and Ribazar Tarz*

ANGELS

The angels are real. They work with you and you work with them. I love the angels and I love you.

– *God*

APPRECIATION

There is a paradox that exists when you are merged with All That Is. Through total appreciation of the moment there is a great power that will flow through you, but you do not direct It and It does not direct you. It is through appreciation that you could live and express in very ordinary ways while at other times the extraordinary manifests itself within and around you. This is a function of how present you allow yourself to be. Presence comes from a total acceptance of what is now and not looking for anything else. So it is a kind of paradox where all that you must do is accept what is.

– *Philos*

❖❖❖

The key is to remember that every experience is precious. When you have found how to enjoy life rather than judge it, then each moment becomes, "How exciting this is," or "How miserable and exciting this is." You find yourself, without knowing how you ever did it, seeing and feeling so much meaning in everything. Joy can arrive and stay when you are so intoxicated, so appreciating the rich feelings here and now that it brings tears to your eyes.

– *Philos*

❖❖❖

The very thing that can keep you from what you want is being focused on your next step. Right now is your next step to being in the present. Otherwise you are keeping what you want away. Release any judgment that what you need is being denied. Instead appreciate and learn from every moment, regardless of what that moment brings.

– *Philos*

ASCENSION

The ascended state is a living organism, which itself advances. When you are consistent in it, it is a state in which struggle ends forever, which is the bottom level of ascension.

– Devorah

❖❖❖

You can ascend by being at peace with right now and being at peace about growing into what you are becoming.

-- Philos

❖❖❖

Ascendant consciousness does not come by trying to rise above your needs. It comes from letting go of trying to control your life to meet your needs. The way that happens is that you become so much a part of the Cosmic Consciousness that the personal gets fulfilled by forgetting about it. People have tried to aspire to that, but none of us have made it through aspiration, only through surrender.

– Sun Bear, Chief Great White Eagle and Great Bear

❖❖❖

Prior to awakening, all ascendant souls thought that their shift would be through a doorway into the Divine to be lifted away from human related concerns. But, everyone has found that at least for some time their care, involvement and compassion for the human condition deepened and intensified beyond all conceivable measure. This is because the human condition, in its ascendant nature, is in fact divine. The human condition is an expression of the Creator, which is unlimited in Its ability to cause awakening in ascendant souls. Awakening is a quantum shift beyond quantifying.

– Astarte

❖❖❖

I would describe ascendancy as the result of living an enlightened life as an enlightened being. If I can help you experience what your ascendancy really means, I would say you embrace infinity and surrender all perceptions of time. Ascendancy deteriorates time as a reality and once that happens, it is as though you have always been ascendant. It will not have seemed like a process. When you are in an infinite place, it is so different from the perceptions of most people in your world. You enter into a miraculous existence.

– Philos

❖❖❖

In the process of ascension, letting go of what you do not want becomes a force that is around you. This is because letting in what you really want also means being willing to let go of what you do not want. The whole key is to experience deep pleasure and deep receptivity, then life seems to happen beyond your control because everything will happen so intensely.

– Devorah

❖❖❖

The ascendant state, a place with no struggle, occurs by being as present to and accepting of the moment as you are able to be by making choices that are wise, gentle, kind and empowered. The more you aim yourself in that direction the freer and freer your spirit becomes to the point that you live without the struggle. Then, because your consciousness is free of the struggle, the universe moves in harmony with you instantly. The moment you receive an impulse or impression toward something that is significant to you, the universe will instantly manifest it. Also, the moment the universe has an intention it would like you to carry out, you will find yourself with the desire to do it. You will just find yourself in the right place at the right time.

To embrace an ascendant state, you must accept whatever is in the moment, which requires facing everything inside of you. To do this you must create much space to just be, then we come in and around you in that space. Some of you may be too busy projecting out into the world when instead you need to be present. We come and help you to be present for whatever surfaces in your consciousness so that you might be in a state of practice. In that practice, if you can let go, you will meet God in some form that you can recognize, but never in the form that you expect.

- Merlin

❖❖❖

Your ascendant nature already exists perfectly in you right now. It is merely covered by other layers of consciousness, which you have developed and cultivated out of your need to survive.

– Dormor

❖❖❖

Do not look for confirmations of whether or not you are ascended. Look instead for the signs that you are in fact ascended, which becomes habit and all other habits end. Each time you recognize your ascendance you affirm your identity and oneness with it, which then changes your experience and puts you deeper in the matrix that creates miracles.

– Philos

❖❖❖

One of the strongest archetypes for ascension remaining in this world is from Yeshua. He is one of the Masters with the greatest following and he has an ascension period forty days after Easter. Those persons oriented toward ascension, who have a personal relationship with Yeshua, have the opportunity to ascend in that period.

– Devorah

❖❖❖

In our world of spirit there is one reality, one law. On earth there are many laws: physical, social, philosophical, cultural, legal, gender oriented and time oriented. You have so many laws I do not know how you can do it; you have to breathe, eat and do so many things. Our one law is love without reason, condition and no matter what. Our law is unreasonable and unconditional love, not based upon how well or poorly one does, right or wrong, good or bad, agreement or disagreement. The more that you become unconditional in your love, the fewer laws you will have to obey in order to exist. You will find yourself increasingly leaving one dimension and find yourself in another. You will not know when or how you got there. This is called ascension.

– Sun Bear

❖❖❖

The process of ascension is a matter of accepting who you are right now as you expand into who you are becoming. Acceptance means rejecting no part of who you are right now, which requires no judgment. Acceptance is one of the primary principles for embracing your healing and ascendant awareness.

Another way of looking at ascension is the process of moving from one state of being, where there is a struggle in your thoughts, to a point where your thinking is free from the struggle. This does not mean that there are no challenging ideas and experiences, but that you do not struggle with the fact that you are challenged. Instead of a struggle, you choose to find a perspective that is gentle, wise and empowered. For a human being, the highest elements of awareness are conscious thought, gentleness, kindness, wisdom, empowerment, compassion and love. The love we speak of is not the emotion love, but it is the source of your higher awareness.

When you are in the practice of choosing love in any challenge, you move from the place in your consciousness that is more bogged down, to the upper regions of your consciousness where there is freedom from struggle. Every action and thought therefore manifests itself more and more quickly because it is not attached to other kinds of energies that slow it down by creating interference. Some have described this to be a miracle or magic that when you have a need it instantly manifests because you are in that place where that need can easily be met and you are in reception of it. You are in that place that is beyond time.

– *Merlin*

❖❖❖

Ascension is a substantial and vital change in your psyche such that you are not the being that you were prior to that time. Such spiritual awakening, or ascension is rarely instantaneous for any soul. In the case of most souls, including the Masters you have heard of except the Buddha's whose was in an instant so to speak, there is a gradual awakening that is educational in nature. That is, your life experiences bring spiritual experiences that create awakening.

– *Yeshua*

❖❖❖

What if you allowed yourself to make a total shift into your ascendant nature now? Why not move all the way completely? Why not let every available obstacle be taken right here and now? Why not make a decision right now to invite your fullest self forward, your most radiant, highest, most complete nature? Let it come forward in your being and feel its peace, its strength. Do not reject it with denial, thinking it might go away or might not come. Just continue your invitation and enjoy whatever little or great part of it comes. Make sure you revel and pleasure in it like a pig in mud, enticing it, seducing it, drawing it forward, encouraging it, compelling it, persuading it, dancing with it, twisting in it, falling into it and enjoying it.

– *Merlin*

❖❖❖

With ascension, you will no longer see yourself as threatened. Even if you did, you would laugh and say, "Oh, look at my finite self feeling threatened by this," and it would be instantly released. There would not be fear attached very long, if at all. Your ability to cope with feeling threatened will come forward and also the ability to instantly transmute it into some other form of usable energy. That could mean taking some action that resolves the fear or utilizing it as an opportunity to further let go. That is where the struggle ends.

Ascension means the end of struggle and the lessening of the period of time needed to transmute energy into something that is a lesson or an advanced condition. As you get better and better at doing this, the time spent in struggle shrinks until every single experience of love or confrontation is experienced exactly the same way. It is welcomed as an opportunity to transmute it or use it for something that benefits you without going through a struggle to get to that point.

– Philos

❖❖❖

There are three levels of commitment to ascension. There are those people who simply love the energy and who love to get infusions. There are those who believe they want to ascend and who are inspired to it, but want someone or something to do it for them. Then there are those who are willing to continually do the inner work necessary: communications with Guides, meditation, inner skill development work, visualizations, recording dreams, becoming lucid and practicing the skills of bilocation. This is the highest level of commitment and we facilitate these people. Let me be clear that these are not a level of spiritual development. I am describing three groups of people. In every group that I have just described there will be all levels of spiritual evolution.

– Dormor

❖❖❖

The steps to ascension may be described as follows. First, getting born and you did that pretty well because here you are. Each time you are born, you are born with all of the cosmic consciousness, everything. Then perhaps some of it is lost trying to cope with the conditions you have been born into because you just want some support for your survival.

The most enlightened of children might understand the conditions around them and not be affected, but the more vulnerable ones may say, "Did I do something wrong?" They will start to examine themselves and wonder what they did that was wrong. In cases that are even more difficult, sometimes there is not the love there on the caretaker's part. Even if there is love there, it is still hard. But, if there is not that love it makes it even harder and the child starts to try to figure out what love is. Love then becomes agreement and approval for the child. If the child cannot create approval, they abandon the parent, but also end up feeling badly about themselves. In these processes, the original cosmic consciousness can somehow get lost.

The second step is reconnecting from that lost state. That is when you begin your search. It is a very confusing stage because an inner voice speaks, whether you recognize it or not. This inner voice begins to introduce you to teachers, like-minded people, writings and so forth that begins the reawakening. But, it is confusing because you find so many different theories, principles and teachings of which you do not know how to make sense.

This reconnecting period can be very short or very long. It can take a week, a day, years or lifetimes to get reconnected. But, from sorting that out you move into a third stage, which is refinement.

Refinement is where you discover what works for you and you hone those skills: meditation, inner practices, intuition and psychic skills. Refinement is all of the work that is necessary to reach the final stage. This phase also can be very short or last for lifetimes. The final stage is ascendancy, where you have refined your awareness and cultivated your being such that you dwell in the place where you continually let go of the struggle.

The fastest route through any of this is the intention to serve because your desire to give is what is expressed through your service. Doorways to the gifts of your spirit then start opening one after the other because you let go into a particular vibration.

All of this is extremely easy and totally effortless. It is so easy that you may not know how to do it. For example, breathing is something you do so much that it is natural. When you try to do something that is natural it is harder to do than something that is unnatural because it already works better without you thinking about it. So, just do the service.

– Sun Bear

ASPIRATION

Many of you have seen something beyond what eyes see and ears hear. What you have noticed has placed an aspiration in your being to see further still, to understand more, to know more. This aspiration must become considerable in order for you to embrace a truth greater than all of the obstacles that stand as a veil between you and that truth. Without a strong aspiration you will find yourself entangled and caught in so many beliefs that do not hold the answer that you seek.

– Dormor and Lao Tzu

ATTACHMENT

It has always been said by many of the teachers and Masters who come through this world that you need detachment, which has often been misunderstood. People erroneously assumed that detachment meant separating from other people, places and things. Detachment is really detachment from that to which you are attached. In other words, you must become detached from the feelings that you find yourself unable to let go of in order to embrace your union with God.

This is not a mental kind of thing. You cannot will yourself free of the way you feel or will yourself into the light that you want. Detachment is a gift such that when you see the need, you can go into the heart of God and say, "Take me, I am willing."

Detachment is not a matter of doing it one time. Wherever you see yourself attached, you must go into the heart of the Great Spirit and say, "Again, I am willing." You may need to do this again and again. Then a gift is given, first sufficiently to get you through what you could not go through before, then far beyond that. It finally becomes an issue you have entirely forgotten because you possess detachment like a gift.

– Chief Great White Eagle and Sun Bear

AVATARS

One is called an Avatar when they have transmuted the cells of their being into the Avatar nature, for the Avatar is a nature. Within the Avatar nature there are different levels of totality of the highest embrace of it. An Avatar can exist as a young child who is unaware of its nature, who cannot take on the teachings of the world and may feel as if he or she does not fit in. That child does not yet feel the power and peace of its nature and cannot yet take it on. Or, an Avatar can be born in a full embrace of their nature, knowing for example, "I do not take on this world for I am here to teach it," and they begin teaching immediately. Furthermore, an Avatar nature can also happen because of one's devotion to the light. When one gives up being other things and is so embracing the ascendant nature, they leave the former nature and enter into the Avatar nature at any level in between the two described.

An Avatar may have a less conscious connection to the universe and may not realize with full potency that they are one with God. They will however know enough so they are not fooled by any device, concern, person or influence that would have them take on a belief that would separate them further from knowing themselves as an Avatar. Thus, they come to be in full recognition of their Avatar nature because their connectedness with God is so great that they have given up all doubts.

– Philos

❖❖❖

The state that Avatars experience so frequently is that they are in love with their existence all the time. Nevertheless, they are not in their highest experience all the time. That is extremely rare amongst Avatars. They are in the habit of recognizing again and again how they are supported. That recognition is their mastery.

– *Philos*

❖❖❖

Avatars are keenly aware that they are both infinite and finite all the time. They never lose touch that they are infinite and therefore are a source of the miraculous in the world. They never lose touch with the fact that they are also finite and therefore, when they encounter signs of their finite nature, they are untroubled by it because the judgment goes away. Furthermore, they are in the state of love and trust and continually finding themselves confirming, affirming and recognizing that they are totally supported by the universe. They have become one with that which generates and therefore they are the source.

– *Philos*

❖❖❖

Because of their devotion to the Source, Avatars open the doorway for others. With the opening of these doorways, Avatars experience a love unlike any other love in the world. This eventually divorces them from the need for the other kind of love that exists in the world and gives them a true love. The true love is on a spiritual or altruistic plane, never on a physical plane and is worked out in a life of caring for others. While for others to try to do this would be fatal to their emotional well-being, for the Avatar it is the only satisfying love.

Meanwhile, the Avatar, just like any other being, at some point will crave a love like other people have since that is what they have known for all their existences prior to that time. Every lifetime that they have experienced a fulfillment of human love on that level, they are confronted by all their attachments to human love of the kind they had experienced prior to that. They begin to experience again the closure, fulfillment or completion of human love after human love of the third dimensional variety while they open to the love of heaven, a fourth-dimensional love. This love worked out on the altruistic plane.

Many people will think they are on that level of spiritual love, only to find that they still have more to work out. Yet again and again, if they are an Avatar and seek to love in the spiritual or altruistic plane, the closer they will get to a more fulfilling love than they had ever known. It has different qualities altogether than the third-dimensional love.

Third-dimensional love will never be denied to an Avatar. They will face the opportunity for third-dimensional style love that will be offered by those in third-dimensional conditioning. The Avatar may choose to take a lover or partner of a third-dimensional reality, but their truest love will always be the love worked out on the altruistic plane. That is a spiritual love that goes far beyond the love of the third-dimensional plane.

– Francesco

❖❖❖

AWAKENING

You are on a journey of awakening to what may take tens of thousands of years for human beings to embrace, but it need not take tens of thousands of years, for it can be today. There is a beautiful thing that transpires when you, the spirit who lives within and around your physical form, shift your awareness into a place called higher self, true self or original self. A very beautiful thing happens to time and space when you make this shift. Your journey then begins to be seen in an eternal context and everything begins to make sense.

When you transcend time and space, you understand why you have gone through what you have gone through and you understand what the road is that lies ahead. Although you may not grasp it all at once on an intellectual level, the core of your being begins to acknowledge and say, "Yes, something is formulating in me. Something is becoming aware. Something is moving, opening."

Then the veils that exist between what you might call your dimension and ours begin to disappear. You will not be able to understand it in terms of your intellectual perceptions or mental grasp and that is the point. You learn how to live in the dimension where we are, by learning how to perceive with another part of your being other than simply your intellect or senses. Your consciousness becomes aware of consciousness Itself.

You are here to learn how to embrace higher consciousness and dwell there. You will live in the miraculous if you are able to touch this place. It is the place where you enter into a circuitry or matrix of energies. In this matrix, the events that transpire in your physical existence begin to be seen and experienced in such a meaningful way that you perceive the universe giving you gifts of help. You see the universe coordinating the events in your life and you find yourself in the right places at the right times. You experience everything that you recognize to be important coming to you and you are not alone anymore. Where there used to be terrible loneliness you experience a union with the Most High, even in your times of sadness and grief as well as in times of joy and ecstasy.

– Merlin

❖❖❖

Awakening is not a question of climbing the spiritual ladder to the top of the spiritual mountain. It is not a question of how many years you have been on the spiritual path, whether it has been thirty years or fifty lifetimes or whether you have simply come here supposedly by accident and think you are in the wrong place. It does not matter.

It is not a matter of length of time because there is not any time. Awakening is a matter of entering a place that is eternal even if you are not able to identify it. The eternal place is something that does not wear a label saying that it is eternal and it is not something that you can get a grasp on. It is merely being yourself and being with whatever is present right now.

- Merlin

❖❖❖

Most awaken and ascend through a gradual process that occurs in stages. These stages result from spiritual experiences and the working out of your problems on an altruistic plane. All human beings are moving into an awakening, yet some so slowly they are wholly unaware of that unfolding. Those who come to see the need to resolve their issues and problems on a spiritual level, as a result of the connection between themselves and the Supreme, ask for guidance and seek utter surrender. As a result they become concerned for the welfare of others. They are therefore working out their problems on an altruistic plane, ultimately leaving behind all self-centered desires and currently existing values.

– Miriam, Quan Yin and Astarte

❖❖❖

When there is devotion to the Supreme and to service, awakening is accelerated. That is to say, all that is valued in the world loses its meaning. Then you are no longer of the world even though you are in the world and in a sense a product of the world.

You live in two worlds, but increasingly your consciousness and concerns come from another dimension. All that is revealed from life experience then is the lesson that all that needs to be worked through is sourced from a higher idea, the Creator. The Creator's essence is found deep, deep within your being, down deep in your heart where there is no longer any impure desire. From that place, from that loving union comes forth all direction and light.

– Miriam, Quan Yin and Astarte

❖❖❖

It takes so many lifetimes to become fully awakened that if you climbed a mountain and scooped a piece of dirt off with a hand shovel once a year, by the time the whole mountain disappeared is how long it would take to become enlightened. You can be very close to that mountain disappearing for a very long time. You can be very close to your last lifetime for thousands of lifetimes. It is not important however, because existence is eternal. Sometimes your mind will set up an arbitrary measure to give your ego some satisfaction. That ego must be taken. Losses occur until all identification with anything that is not original to your soul's nature is gone. Then, what was called a loss is experienced as a burden being lifted and taken away.

– Miriam

BAGGAGE

In your evening meditations, examine where anxiety got a hold of you or where you might have hurt someone with your own wounds. When this is shown to you say, "Great Spirit, heal me of this condition and give them what they need. Give me the willingness and power to right any wrongs." The Great Spirit will give you an inspiration to set things right and something magical will come out of you. That is your footwork and it clears your baggage.

– Sun Bear

BECOMING A LOVER WITH THE UNIVERSE

Becoming a lover of the universe is born of a kind of prayer and devotional back and forth energy. You start letting your feelings out into the universe and receiving responses back, feeling yourself comforted.

– Sun Bear

BEING IN LOVE

Feelings of being in love are your feelings. Because they are your feelings, they are there inside of you all the time. If you are not in love, the reason is that you just will not let those feelings up.

Once your soul is totally open, it starts to feel completely in love with many people for all kinds of reasons. When you are in love in the right way and with your right partner, you will feel like you are in love with many other people too.

– Philos

BEING RIGHT

Be willing to be wrong again and again because there is always something to learn outside of your current understanding. Always be ready to let go of something you believe or have understood. Greatness and love come from being willing to back off and continuously listen and receive. Even if you have a good intention to love but you are always looking to be right, you will lose your ability to love.

When you have been hurt so much you want the pain to stop, you will seek perfection and correctness all the time as an antidote. Without knowing it you will become self-righteous, arrogant, distant and unfeeling. That is the process by which you become unteachable. It is very important that this lesson be looked at. It is not about getting it right; it is about understanding the flow and being willing to learn.

If you are always focused on God, the higher light and all that comes from the Source, then it is always easy to learn. But if you somehow think that it is a person or circumstance you have to learn from, even though the lessons may come through those things, it gets hard to be humble. You then do not want to be taught by a person, a Spirit or by life circumstance. When you realize that your attention is on the Creator, you say, "Fine, if the Creator has a lesson for me I will learn from it." Then you will find it will be so beautiful.

– Devorah

BEING TESTED

The universe is a little bit ruthless. It tests people. It is not because the universe wants to make certain that people are good enough per se. Rather it is because entities cannot survive in the matrix of light unless they are possessed of the qualities of the light, otherwise they will disintegrate, dematerialize, rupture or fracture. For example, the sun is a very beautiful thing, very warming and nurturing. It is also ruthless from a human perspective, for if one goes too close to the sun, it will burn.

– Sun Bear

BEING WHO YOU ARE

The purpose of living is not all that you have amassed and accumulated in terms of accomplishment, recognition and gifts. The purpose is simply to be who you are. When you do everything right and things still happen to go wrong, you will still be who you are. That is the passing of the test. I do not mean passing as though you are graduating and issued rewards. The passing I mean is an experience that occurs within you where the outer world simply does not matter as much to you anymore. It cannot hurt you and you do not fear it.

This state of being is an arrival, an initiation, an accomplishment. It does not come from simply working at it or aspiring to it. It is an achievement in the sense that it is a matter of holding your center because you see that is what matters. The center is where you keep loving and receiving Spirit and yourself, which are one. Spirit sends things to you that support you so that you can keep loving and receiving love.

At the point when love is the only thing you care about, then fear holds no power over you anymore. In place of fear there comes a rush of excitement. Sometimes that excitement itself is a little bit intimidating, but not threatening. Sometimes that rush is a sense that all of the love in the universe is about to come into you to manage the circumstances that have just arrived. This is not a mental experience, but an actual visceral fact that turns your being into a world of joy.

– Philos

BILOCATION

If you wish to develop astral projection and its further extension of bilocation, trilocation and multiple location, work on lucidity in the dream state. You will need to capture about two to four dreams in writing per week and be willing to work on this level for a minimum of six months. You will need to understand the meaning, theme and messages of these dreams.

When you understand the messages the understanding will come more and more quickly, even while you are amidst the dream because your consciousness will learn to be in an interpretative mode. This will follow into your waking life as well. Then within the dream you will begin to notice things that stand out, that let you know you are dreaming. During the dream you will start awakening, recognizing that this is a dream. You will become lucid in that half awake state.

This state of lucidity will allow you to choose the dimension in which to travel the higher planes if you wish. Only when you are lucid are you able to journey consciously in these other dimensions and draw your physical essence into these other dimensions.

Over the course of six months attempt to practice many overnight meditations. Nothing brings lucidity more quickly than that. During your waking state, check reality. For example, jump to see if you fly. This way if you do not fly, you know you are in a waking state. If this becomes a practice, you will also do that in your dreaming state.

Sometimes you may wish to go to bed thirsty. Do not drink anything after a certain time and place a glass of water at a particular point in another room. On the nights you practice dream recall, intend to travel to that water. Thirst is a very compelling drive and you will think about that water when you are thirsty. That pull will draw you out of your body to the water and get you to linger by that water. Prior to sleeping you may wish to stand by the water and program yourself to come there in astral form. Then as you lay in bed after meditating, you can say, "I will journey to the water and will become lucid when I arrive there."

These steps are where you may begin the practices to help you develop bilocation. Do not do this every night because sometimes you simply need to journey where your soul needs to go without having an agenda.

– Dormor

BOREDOM

If you find yourself restless and bored say, "Creator, please point me in the direction of service." Ask the Creator to entwine Itself and show you the way. It is the continuing rapport between you and the Great Spirit that will keep bringing you pleasure and excitement every single day.

– Chief Great White Eagle, Olga and Helga

CHANGE

Only that which is willing to change is infinite. Anything that exists without change is a stagnant pool and it stinks! You are here in this dimension learning how to embrace change graciously, using each other as support. You are seeking to touch the aliveness that is your spirit and develop an intimacy with your true being. When you know yourself on that level, then everything in life is an adventure.

How can you survive in an existence where everything is changing all of the time? It is very easy if you stop trying to prevent things from changing. It is the nature of the mind to try to make everything like a computer. I know your computers have made you very smart, but the tendency is to try to make everything fit into what you imagine you would like it to be. Reality is not like that.

– Motambi Motombi (Mo)

CHOICES

The more you enter your mastery the more you notice that the choices are between two good things instead of a good thing and a crisis. It should be that your choices are surrounded by opportunity.

– Sun Bear, Chief, Tall Trees, Two Trees, Sky Walker, Sam Strong Body, Red Sky and many others

❖❖❖

As an old, wise soul you may come to see that you do not have as many choices as you thought. Life for you may not really seem to be as free as for many others. When a new soul comes here the whole universe is open to them, but the older a soul is, the more focused on the finishing of their business they become.

– Yeshua and Ribazar Tarz

CLAIRVOYANCE

Seeing clairvoyantly is not a physical function. However, when you begin to see clairvoyantly you think it is physical. Physical seeing is also not a physical function; you just see what you are able to conceptualize. What you are unable to conceptualize in your mind's eye, your physical eyes will never see. That is, when you look at things that are not within the paradigm of your understanding you will not even see them.

Seeing is a function of expanding consciousness, of growing awareness that goes hand in hand with the ability to be present. That kind of seeing takes place with your third eye where things in other dimensions begin to appear to you visually and you begin to understand them. When those visuals begin to happen understand that they are going on in your consciousness and not in your eyeballs. If you begin to look through your physical eyes your third eye will turn off. It is all a matter of being willing to practice allowing your consciousness to become aware. Clairvoyance is a different kind of seeing.

– Kira

COMPASSION

Compassion is the aspect of love that makes love unconditional and it allows a loving being to identify with another being. It is compassion that causes a soul to reach out past their own experience or self-centered concerns however real, justified, distracting or compelling those concerns might be. The aspect of love called compassion allows all thought of self to disappear and a universal presence appears in its stead. Forgetting personal concerns unites a person with truth that then lifts the personal concerns. Such a person then becomes more enlightened by that state.

– *Miriam*

COMPLETING

When a being comes into this life and is willing and prepared to complete their business there are many difficult closures to be made. So many closures to be made in fact that by the time you reach a point where you have the wish to complete your existence here, it is so tremendously challenging that it usually takes hundreds of lifetimes after that before you actually have the necessary willingness and capacity to complete. Systematically you will make closure with so many affairs that it feels as if you are all alone and that nobody understands.

It is indeed a rigorous path that requires absolute commitment to love and to the sense of resolution, which can only come about with the acquisition of the quality of serenity, a by-product of the journey. Time and again on such a journey you will realize that the magnitude of what you embark upon is so large, awesome and magnificent that the only thing you find yourself able to do is humbly rest in the hands of the Supreme, which dwells within and all around you.

Eventually a core of devotion exists between you and the Supreme that is so potent you cannot tell the difference between yourself and the Supreme. It is like an infant who is so identified with its mother that she thinks she is the mother and the mother thinks she is the child because such a bond of love and devotion exists.

-- *Francesco*

❖❖❖

In the business of completing, you cannot seek the same things others seek, which is why you may feel so alone. But, you are not here doing the same things as others. By moving forward, seeking to connect with the Spirit, to serve the Higher Will and complete, miracles will occur around you that do not happen with other people. As a result of this energy being created within and around you many others, who could not be saved from the tortures of their lives, will be lifted through the doorway.

– Francesco

❖❖❖

When a soul is in completion, it is a completion of the final affairs of their human life, not of their existence.

– Francesco

COMPLICATIONS

Every area of your life has so many complications, actions and reactions that you are much better just saying daily, "Creator, I know that I do not know, so I need an intuitive thought or sign about how to proceed this day. And while you are at it, take from me all that I seem to get into that stands in the way. I am tired of it." Then the problem just gets diminished enough that you can get on with your day. If you have enough of those days, your existence becomes very beautiful.

– Merlin

CONNECTEDNESS

What is necessary is to spend time cultivating a gut and a heart that are able to recognize yourself as a part of everyone and everything and everything and everyone as a part of you. There is nobody below you and nobody above you because everybody is right there in the crowd with you. Everybody else is where your lessons are. In this way you find yourself as a part of everything rather than apart from everything.

– Chief Great White Eagle, Sun Bear, with Miriam

❖❖❖

If you do not have connection, you can feel very threatened and vulnerable. Then when things happen around you there will be the tendency to judge yourself by what good is happening or what bad is happening. In fact, the light force you are is greater than everything that can happen to you.

The way is found by seeing yourself as one with everything. You can experience support, give support and see everybody as in a web supporting each other. You are just a part of that web. That is what will reveal to you the true nature of your soul, which you will not find through the aspiration to achieve a particular end. Aspiration will only lead to disappointment, disillusionment or promise after promise that never seems to come true.

– Chief Great White Eagle, Sun Bear and Miriam

CONNECTION WITH THE SUPREME

There is a steep and heavy price to pay for those who wish to become a part of the light: an absolute and total surrender, letting go of all elements of consciousness that stand in the way of the embracing of the light. Thus historically, relatively few have been able to do this, instead finding themselves greatly invested in the affairs of the earth and in their own personal desires related to that involvement. Or, they have found themselves unable or unwilling to clear away what has become integrated into their psyches that they have grown very attached to throughout their earth incarnations. These attachments within the psyche have to be given up because they have so integrated that the person has developed a spiritual personality that they presume is the nature of the truth.

Surrender into the light ultimately requires a contact with the Supreme that is so certain that it is greater than everything else. The contact must be greater than relationship, sex, power, any other ambition and everything else. If everything goes away you will know that because of your own connection with the Supreme you are in the right place.

- Chief Great White Eagle

CONSCIOUSNESS

You are not your physical body. You just happen to have a body. Your body is a very vital, important part of you, but it is certainly not all of you. You are consciousness itself.

– Motambi Motombi (Mo)

❖❖❖

In this existence it is impossible to entirely be a power unto yourself. The nature of consciousness and of your being is to want to mingle with other energies, people, situations, circumstances and forces around you. That is why no one can stand being alone all the time. Some may need alone time some of the time, but nobody can stand the idea of being alone for all time because consciousness needs interaction with other consciousness.

The great reason why there is a compelling need to be in agreement with something is because your consciousness functions best like a cog in a wheel. If that wheel is turning by itself, it feels incomplete, but if it is integrated with other things, there is a sense of purpose.

– Motambi Motombi (Mo)

❖❖❖

As you expand, many of you will find it a challenge to still relate to the world around you. You will find that expanded awareness seems not to be accepted by the consensus that exists around you. Your motivations will become different, values will shift, orientations will change, beliefs will alter and that which you previously knew as self goes through change and even disruption. As you go through disruption, your seeking of what is in fact spiritual awareness shall inevitably lead you to challenge yourself and the very spiritual awareness you have sought.

– Dormor

CONSENSUS THINKING

It is very good to get together in the company of your spiritual peers. Without that you will think you are crazy in this world. What is crazy anyway? You must learn to accept it if somebody says you are very strange. You must learn to say, "Thank you, I try!" This is very true because unless you are willing to get outside of the consensus thinking, you will have a life that is destined to mediocrity. Excellence, wisdom and genius occur outside of the limits of your beliefs.

– Motambi Motombi (Mo)

CONTRIBUTING

You can generate many kinds of support in the world for yourself: financial, romantic, health, and others. You can acquire a certain level of mastery in those ways. But, the time comes when there is a part of your being that craves profound contribution and a significant purpose that are so meaningful to you that you are in ecstasy to be alive. This you cannot create because it only comes from Great Spirit and it must be asked for. You can create many things, but this one you cannot create.

When you ask for it, Great Spirit will always say yes. Then the journey begins and it usually begins with, "Well, now what? I asked and I feel the sense of a yes, but what do I do?" Sometimes Great Spirit just communicates, "Wait. Stay right there until I return," whatever that means. It may feel like Great Spirit has forgotten you, but when Great Spirit returns, Great Spirit wants you there because when your time comes you will be needed. Great Spirit says, "Fine, you asked and the answer is yes. Now let me find the place."

Great Spirit may need to create the space in two ways: one for you to be in and the other in you so that you are ready. If you resist, the whole flow will stop until another place can be found for you. In the meantime you will need to get more ready.

It is a serious and beautiful thing to embrace the reality of what you have asked for. Be prepared to have it delivered to your door immediately. Be prepared to act on the tiniest presentation that comes to you.

The beautiful thing about responding to the tiny presentations is that then the rest will start. We will all take many steps toward you. We are just as willing to focus what we are through what you want as we are willing to have you focus your energy to our intention. We have no jealousy, no envy with sharing the gift of light and power. We do not want to possess this, but instead want to give it. Great Spirit wants to deliver everything that It has to focus through you, everything without a limit. Our trust, Great Spirit's trust in you is total, complete. Why shouldn't it be? What is there to fear? So receive it.

– *Merlin*

CONTROL

Life is like the ocean. Can you imagine thinking that in order to enjoy yourself you had to control the whole ocean? It is a very powerful ocean with a great deal to show you. If you try to make it work for you, you will miss the whole point. You must let it show you things, learning to ride with its currents and tides. You do not need to control it to enjoy it.

– Merlin

❖❖❖

You are not in charge and you need to stop trying to be. What is in charge is life and it is bigger than you.

– Sun Bear, Chief, Tall Trees, Two Trees, Sky Walker, Sam Strong Body, Red Sky and many others

❖❖❖

Most older souls find themselves in some kind of service work. At a point some of them even find themselves tired of doing it or resistant to it, even though they are doing the very thing for which they came. Sometimes older souls are secretly seeking control over their environment so they often have a great deal of resistance. When they are actually offering the thing they are here to offer they find themselves becoming free and that never goes away. The tiredness comes from secretly looking inside for that control that will give them the way to be free forever. They do not yet understand that their freedom is from passing on the light.

– Merlin

❖❖❖

The universe makes you deal with anything that is out of balance or out of integrity.

– Sun Bear, Chief, Tall Trees, Two Trees, Sky Walker, Sam Strong Body, Red Sky and many others

❖❖❖

You cannot conform to what is right according to Spirit. Instead, the Spirit of the Universe has to get a hold of you and free you from your fears and doubts. That will put you into harmony with It. As long as you are trying to move or control anything, it will not work.

– Sun Bear, Chief, Tall Trees, Two Trees, Sky Walker, Sam Strong Body, Red Sky and many others

❖❖❖

Very little of the voice of Spirit can be heard in the face of your spiritual aspirations and goals or even your world goals. You must be ready to put all ambitions aside and truly say to the spirit of God Itself, "I am here that you may show me the reason for which I live, not here to direct You as to how to fulfill me."

– Miriam, Isis, Quan Yin

COURAGE

To grow requires absolute courage. There is no movement forward without it. You do not have to be totally courageous all the time, but to grow you have to find absolute courage at some point or another and faith leads you to that point. Faith does not need to be grand. It can be very small, but it can lead to great courage.

– Philos

❖❖❖

You must have the courage to follow your vision without the expectation that even somebody you love has the same vision as you.

– Devorah, Helga and Olga, Nemo

CRAVINGS

You must ask the Spirit of the Universe not to let your cravings control what is right for you. The Creator will put the cravings in balance for you and you will be able to cope with what goes on. The right things will result as your life is put into order for you. But, if you try to make those arrangements yourself, you will inevitably make big mistakes and a different result will occur.

– Sun Bear, Chief, Tall Trees, Two Trees, Sky Walker, Sam Strong Body, Red Sky and many others

CREATING

Anyone who appears to be creating reality in exactly the way they intended it is creating an image for others to see and holding it up while inside there is huge emptiness. The ones who truly say you can create reality as you want it, who really use their power to create that will tell you, "You know, it fell apart a thousand times before it got there." They will have a story of real wisdom.

It takes personal power to create reality in the way that you want it. But life is the best teacher and shows you how to be flexible. You have to let go of a thousand ideas a thousand times. It comes about because you hold an intention and then let the universe show you the way. The real Masters tend to speak like that.

– Sun Bear, Chief, Tall Trees, Two Trees, Sky Walker, Sam Strong Body, Red Sky and many others

CREATOR

The Creator of all is a broad and vast consciousness that dwarfs everyday concerns because of its vastness. The Infinite can hardly regard the concerns of your daily existence as material to your destiny. The Infinite only acknowledges an entity who seeks surrender into Its Sourceness, into Its Godness and in so doing becomes an agency through which light can pour.

– Philos

DARKNESS

When your dark side is fully accepted, it is disempowered and the charge is taken out of it. That is when there is no more fear of any dark side from anyone or anything. That is when no person, place, circumstance or anything external to you is a threat to any aspect of your being. There is no threat when you are comfortable with your own light and own dark, and they walk hand in hand forward into life.

– Chief Great White Eagle and Sun Bear

❖❖❖

The presence of the shadow or dark side is an inexplicable anomaly that occurs simultaneously with the light even in the most awakened souls. Therefore, it has often been said that the Avatar or the awakened soul walks a path between heaven and hell, darkness and light. The two are hand in hand, but the charge is absolutely gone in the awakened soul and there is a healthy respect for the dark side.

In the most enlightened souls, great gratitude exists for the dark side because they know that it has allowed them to embrace the magnificent light. Time and time again their dark side has revealed to them such magnificence that they respect it as their greatest teacher. They welcome the presence of their shadow self as an important part of their entire being.

This is how the Creator Itself embraces all of Its nature. The Creator has a loving and profound receptivity of Its own dark side. It is in this way that it can be said that human beings are made in the likeness of God.

– Astarte

❖❖❖

You do not eradicate the dark side to live in the light. You become powerful by ceasing to fight your dark side. You cannot get there when you are trying to control everything because that is the fight. Instead you come to live with and respect your dark side and you no longer fear it. You realize that you are frail as well as powerful. When there is acceptance, the fight with your dark side stops.

– Merlin

❖❖❖

Aspects of darkness are things like fear, dishonesty, manipulation, self-centeredness and selfishness. When you see these things creating demands in your being and the demands are not getting addressed, do not ask for their fulfillment. Ask instead to be saved from your demands, freed from the burden of these strong desires. Ask to give up these things.

All fear is tied into holding onto these demands, trying to create fulfillment, which leaves the fears that underlie these demands never getting addressed. The fear is that if these demands are given up you can never be happy, but it is the fear that creates discontent. The fears must be given daily to the Supreme to be lifted until you are truly, truly free. Freedom from these demands allows you to live in the light.

You cannot be free of the demands simply to be free of them. You get free by submitting the fear-based demands of your will, which drive all motivations toward your own needs, to the Source. When you remove these drives by the will of the Divine so that you can better serve, then these drives are lifted in the name of that service. At that time you begin to know serenity. In the serenity, your will is guided by other motivation than by the need to survive. There is a desire to be embraced by the light that you have received, to touch others with that light and to watch the glow that others have as they too are freed from their inner burdens. Passing on the light becomes the way you find freedom.

– Astarte and Miriam

❖❖❖

Be not afraid of the darkness, for it holds the promise of the light. For as surely as the sun rises and sets, so too shall the earth see the dawn of a new day.

– *Yeshua*

DEATH

It is said that when the body dies all that dies is the body, but the spirit lives on. That is not entirely true, for indeed something far more than the body is left behind. Within the body are many manifestations and expressions of the psyche. When the body dies, vast parts of the psyche die along with the body. Hence, there is a sense of freedom at the time of death, for many of the restricting forms of psyche that are also held within the body are utterly and entirely left behind. Indeed so much so, that the remaining spirit can have a powerful and dynamic psychic change. The change can be so intense and thorough that many times, even after a short time, the entity is entirely unrecognizable by those whom they left behind. Then, when a communication is necessary, the one who has translated into another dimension must recover many elements of the psyche they left behind in order to be recognizable.

There are some who, upon the crossing, entirely resist any sort of change. These souls suffer greatly. If they indulged in the cultivation of ego, particularly negative ego, in the course of their lifetime, they experience a true hell. Resistance to a great and powerful universal force requires strong and willful abiding attachment to that which is unreal. Thus, a number of experiences manifest that are completely subject to that entity's own fears or dark side. Therefore, it is to great advantage to begin letting go of ego and embracing the light long before translating into the higher dimension.

– *Yeshua*

❖❖❖

There is really no such thing as time, just right timing. Time is the sense of urgency, of need without fulfillment, that there is presumably something to do before it is too late, or that you will die.
There are two ways to handle death: either accept you are never going to die or accept that you will. Either way relinquishes time and kills the urgency. There really is no need for urgency because you cannot truly die.

Time must disappear because the perception of time stands in the way of who you are. How do you let perceptions of time disappear? Do you remember past lives or perhaps little bits or feelings, or a sense that you may have lived before? See. Death did not work. You cannot remember death because all that happens at the time of death is that you leave your body. At which point did you cease existence? See. It did not work. You remember exiting the body, but you do not remember ceasing existence do you? Of course you do not. Do you remember beginning existence? You have no memory here either? This is very interesting.

Even in this life, do you remember your first moment of cognizance? If you remember it, you must have been there for it. In other words, you must have been cognizant at the time. You must have been aware first, and then had the experience. If you had the experience and were not aware, you would not remember it. You have to have awareness before you can remember. So the awareness must have been there first, and then the experience you can remember. That is the first memory of experience.

What I am trying to say is, I do not know where people get the idea that they begin and end. If they were there, present for their death, they obviously were not ended. If they were there for some first remembrance, they obviously did not begin there. You have hallucinated that you begin and end, and for the most part you agree on it. It is not true and you do not do it. It is very much like dreams for example, or dreams are very much like life until you awaken from them.

Have you had dreams of being murdered or killed or dying? You may wonder if they are past life memories, but let us call them dreams for a moment. Do you remember what you did at that moment when it became too terrifying? You woke up. You had some control over it, did you not? And this is why you have a death urge and a life urge.

Everyone has both an urge to live and an urge to die. They are really urges for the same thing, to wake up. When you want to die it means you are trying to get out of the dream, break through and wake up. Do not fear death. Go with it. Do not fear life. Go with it. Both life and death lead to waking up.

Some people are terribly afraid of their death urge, feeling that they are going to get into an accident or kill or destroy themselves. Some people are afraid they will destroy other things. It is very common for new mothers for example, to be afraid they are going to kill their child with their irresponsibility or forgetfulness. They are afraid they will roll over on them when they fall asleep or they will drop them. Many fathers will not even touch children because they are afraid they will break them. Now this is not fear of the child's death, but fear of their own destructiveness. They fear that they may kill or hurt themselves and they project it onto the child.

You might look around and see other people suffering, dying, being born and somehow you convince yourself, "I must have begun. I will die and I can suffer." That really does not make much sense because there are many other choices that can be made. Utilize being here to wake up forever.

How do you utilize it to do that? Just decide it. Make a decision. Do you know what a decision is? A decision is accepting no other reality than the one you prefer. You rule out the things you do not prefer. Now you say, "How can I do that?" Well if you do not prefer it, should it not be easy? Why is it difficult to make a decision about something you want and to rule out what you do not want? Why is it easier to make a decision that what you do not want will be, and what you do want, will not? You see, somehow you get spun by being here. You must get unspun. Some of the work we do with you is exactly that.

– Merlin

DEMONS

Holding awareness of your own demons makes you accessible to love. From deep self-examination and becoming safe with the darkness you will become invulnerable to demons, for they shall put down their weapons before you.

Dishonesty with yourself about your motives leads to a failure to comprehend the level of your own self-centeredness and control, which keeps it in motion. To notice your self-centeredness and control, do a review each night. Ask yourself where your motivations have been self-centered that day and ask God for intervention. This will disempower the darkness.

– Astarte and Miriam

DENIAL

There are dimensions of experience that human beings have where they deny parts of themselves. That is not acceptable to me. If I cannot show you how to change that, then I shall send the angels and the saints in the physical and nonphysical dimensions of the world so that you can be taught how to be accepting of all parts of yourself.

– God

DESIRE

There are many pictures born of need and fear that form in your consciousness and masquerade as the promise of a gift. These are simply urges of your lower self that ground you to death and mortality. Indeed, it takes great love and great trust to let go and find out what exists beyond your own particular desire or intention. You shall be advanced by the surrendering of your desire into the intent of a loving Creator's intent for you.

Great love or trust comes through the gift of serenity that is then given. Ask for serenity to be given to you so that you can meet with your worldly life, needs, desires and obligations. Through that serenity there comes a great and powerful joy or love that entirely orients your spirit into a higher dimension. It is a dimension where you are in the same state of being that is embraced at the time of your translation from the physical world. This is called ascension, enlightenment or awakening.

– *Yeshua*

❖❖❖

Desires are of two minds. One is the kind of aspiration that creates angst or longing, which pulls you toward a higher destination. The other is that the desire creates either a possibility or impossibility that it can be fulfilled. Either extreme, the possibility or the impossibility, reflects the desire and blocks the possibility of something existing beyond that intention. Therefore, all desire must be surrendered so you may be taken beyond into a more awakened state.

– *Astarte*

❖❖❖

When you have made a decision to surrender, strong desires must be acknowledged and left entirely to the vast Spirit of the Universe to address. Otherwise, the power of those desires, flowing in directions other than altruism, will cause a great crashing in your personal life. That power, if directed by the vast Spirit, which you are part of, will cause a great lifting or ascension.

Do not develop strong desires for that which exists in this world. You will have enough desires without developing more. Do not cultivate existing desires, but simply ask the Spirit to address them. Desires are not wrong or bad to have. In fact, many of them are quite good, but if you cultivate the existing strong desires, you will be taken away from your truest focus. Your power will be focused in ways that will set things atumble.

– *Yeshua*

❖❖❖

The pointers to your destiny will not come from, "What am I supposed to do?" Rather they come from, "How can I be of service?"

– Chief Great White Eagle

DEVOTION

I have given you the privilege of separating from Me if you choose, and the privilege of joining Me if you choose. Both are good. Now I want something from you. I want your devotion and I want your undying love.

– God

❖❖❖

When you are devoted to spirituality, light and service, and someone else who is not devoted gets confused by your life, they are supposed to! You are the living example of a new way and this spreads the light. Your constant prayer of, "Use me in the way that is right because I cannot even see what works," forms your relationship with Great Spirit. Trust comes from the relationship and from the trust comes joy. Your life will then have far reaching effects that you do not even know about.

– Chief Great White Eagle, Olga and Helga

DIMENSIONS

Dimensions are not stacked on top of each other, but instead all interpenetrate each other. We are here amongst you and you are amongst us. We are all here together. It is just that the 'here' we are seeing is a little different, but we are all here together, including The Great Spirit.

Use us. We are real. Give us your pain and we will give you peace. Give us the suffering and we will help lift you into your light. Give us your sadness and we can show you where the joy is. That is why we come. We are devoted to love.

– Sun Bear

❖❖❖

The astral dimension is similar to the physical in many respects, just more etioplastic; it moves faster so when you think it becomes. Here you think and it becomes, but it takes longer. The higher the dimension the faster and more etioplastic so that form, time and space becomes meaningless at some point. You need time and space only in the denser dimensions where there is a journey from one point to another. In the lighter dimensions you become omnipresent; there is no journey, no point between here and there.

The higher the dimension you go into, the harder it can be to retain the experience because most of your memory is contained in sensory perception. Strong senses, visions, feelings, sounds, colors and perceptions are easier to retain. You lose that as your memory finds it harder to hold onto perceptions. Thus, you must lose that part of your being that absorbs experience sensorially as you enter into higher dimensions. You absorb experience instead through awareness or consciousness rather than through sensory perception.

In the astral dimension there is still a good deal of sensory awareness. Indeed astral is the source of your sensory perceptions, emotions and physical feelings. Sometimes as you go through the dimensions there are different kinds of functioning that are needed to embrace what goes on there. You must make the journey many times to discover what part of yourself perceives in those lighter dimensions.

When you are in that place of entwining with the Cosmic Will, your will and Cosmic Will are one. Cosmic Intention becomes your intention. There is no other decision that can be made but that. No other reality can exist for you but that one.

If you have issues of power and powerlessness you cannot go into this dimension until you first handle those issues. You will handle those issues in relationships where you learn how to be your own power and learn about certain giving and taking in whatever ways you need. When you are ready, you will go to the higher place. Then, when the will speaks inside to you, that is the only reality that can exist for you.

– *Dormor*

❖❖❖

The depth and context do not exist in this dimension that can properly hold the consciousness and substance of the higher dimension. Only a tiny part of it can come forward into your world. This distortion or refraction can be very confusing to those of your dimension. That is why it is so necessary for those who reach to the higher dimensions and serve as a matrix to be possessed of great faith. It is their faith that creates the context for a higher reality to demonstrate in their life so that others may see.

The very world that is the higher dimension is real for those possessed of that faith. Those not possessed of that faith, cannot hold the context for it to appear, but they can see it in those who are able to hold that context. They can learn from those who have that faith, then the world that is that higher dimension can appear in their life also. They may then see the work of the Creator and the higher dimension more in their own life. The higher dimension then has another anchor into this one.

– Yeshua and Milarepa

❖❖❖

There are doorways, if you can find them, that are points or warps. They are a shifting of dimensions by which you can cross into other dimensions without traveling through distance. Through the doorways of consciousness you can go into the place of infinity, which means journeying into many different kinds of universes and dimensions. These dimensions are infinite and they are also access points into other physical universes.

– Dormor

❖❖❖

The very fabric of space and time is important to understand in some literal ways such that you are able to trust the experiences that unfold within and around you. For example, look at a picture. Let us assume that the picture is a being that exists in a two-dimensional world. You are a being in a three-dimensional world. If you wished to reveal yourself to that two-dimensional being, perhaps you would lay your hand upon its world where it could perceive the flatness of your hand. But, it could not perceive the rest of you or the depth of your hand because it can only perceive two dimensions, the width and length of your hand.

If you wished to reveal more of yourself, you would have to turn your hand around many times and still the two-dimensional being could not grasp the whole picture. The being would only see changing shapes and forms, but not really what you are. It would be able to deduce a certain amount about what you might be like, but all that would be visible would be incomprehensible changing shapes and forms.

If you were to reveal a small box to the world of that two-dimensional being, you would have to make it flat to reveal six panels. When you folded it back up into a box, one of the panels would seem to disappear. The two-dimensional being could not comprehend the whole box. Similarly, if you were to have a box in your world, the parallel to that box in the fourth dimension would create a kind of hyper-cube. It would be impossible for you to imagine a fourth-dimensional box because it would be invisible to you.

If we were to unfold that box, instead of six panels you would see six cubes. But as we began to fold those parts of the box back up into a fourth-dimensional box, each cube would seem to disappear until the only thing that would appear in your world would be a box. Inside that box would be six other cubes or panels that would represent the other dimensions.

If you were to enter into that box, you would become aware of a hyper-dimensional world, but you would experience it differently than we experience it. For example, if you were to peer out of the window of that hyper-cube, you might see the ocean in the sky, China outside of your home or the planet Venus. This is because time and space are very altered from a multidimensional space. As you go higher and higher into dimensions that are more and more inclusive of reality, the world seems to take on a different proportion.

The reason you live in a world where all dimensions are not observable is because the earth itself is in a warp. The fabric of space and time where planets exist warps space and time such that it is not really what you might call reality. Your scientists have recognized this by sending clocks into space and having the clocks return with a different time than the clocks on earth.

The relationship of space and time outside of the warp that earth is in is very different. In fact, the future and past as you know it is all going on at once as well as many parallel realities. But here in this warp, as in any warp that exists on any planet, things appear to be different.

Your consciousness is a being that does not dwell within the time and space warp of the earth even though your physiological body and whole life are involved with a world that lives in that warp. Hence, you experience a duality that is greatly, greatly strange and impossible to figure out. The way that you must live, versus the truth of existence itself, is very different. Indeed, this is what creates so much discontent, deep depression and confusion in the case of many inspired beings in all fields.

Since awareness comes from an inspired being's ability to reach beyond the warp into reality, embrace it and make it meaningful and comprehensible to those of their dimension, in most cases these beings have been unsuccessful in the world's context. Some have been left to struggle greatly in the physical world, having no means of drawing the necessary media that makes their consciousness relatable to people of their day and time. By and far, such beings have suffered. Those who have gone insane have lacked faith and have become unsuccessful in order to survive, some becoming tyrannical or confused leaders of their day. Without the ability to draw completely understandable linear links between a multiplicity of dimensions of which they are aware and their world is not aware, they have been unable to find harmony.

The spiritual experience is the experience that enables you to notice peculiar understandings that give meaning to your life thereby reducing your fear and increasing your trust. As you seek what is in fact the spiritual experience, your states of trust intensify and increase with each experience. If you are willing to let go of the fear or to give your fear less meaning, then your fears diminish. You are then able to function as a higher-dimensional being in states of faith and less like a lower-dimensional being in states of fear.

These spiritual experiences must be sought and are not always comprehended. You must use your gifts to be happy and let the light flow through you. Never does enough flow through you that you are fully able to understand yourself or your purpose, but just enough to create enough faith to learn, grow, be free, happy and full of joy.

You must seek a simple, not an expansive existence. Otherwise, your views of an expansive existence will create pain and suffering because being of a three-dimensional world, your understandings of an expansive vision will be totally confused, misguided, and misinterpreted. In the same way, if a being of a two-dimensional world thought it comprehended a three-dimensional world just because it had visions given it that were only parts and pieces of your world it would be sorely mistaken. The pieces of the picture you had shown this being would be an extraordinarily tiny part of what is. Even so, this two-dimensional being would have seen a lot more than the rest of its flatland world had seen.

The fact that the two-dimensional being knows a little, does not mean that they can see nearly enough of the three-dimensional world to know that world. Only that flatland being of a two-dimensional world who can trust that they do not know will be open enough to keep receiving more. Those beings who think they do know will then be bound to use their limited awareness in very confusing ways that do not work.

The perspective of openness and, "I don't know," leaves time to be shown more and more and more and every day then becomes the revelation of the spiritual experience. The one who tries to take the expansive but extremely limited experience and base a life upon it, thinking that is enough, will find themselves instead moved by fears and limited knowledge, which keep them from experiencing joy.

You move through life happily to the extent that you can embrace faith. Faith does not mean the belief that everything is all right. Faith means openness everywhere to the spiritual experience. Those who do not have the awareness of higher dimensions might be able to see clearly enough to arrange their life in such ways as can produce their needs in an average, ordinary and normal way. Their consciousness has not been altered by visions that cause their awareness to be more complete but more confused. Those who open to the higher dimensions need a new power to guide them through existence. That new power is connected to through trust.

– Isis and Miriam

DISRUPTION

Disruptions that occur are not a sign of enlightenment or a lack of it, rather they are an opportunity to ground. It is not that you must grow into a place where there are no disruptions in order to know you are at one. Rather, you start to always remember to access the highest and relink with it. Mastery is coming from that place of empowerment with the oneness. When you are unable to do this, you simply deliver what is too much into the hands of the Source. This is something that never changes.

You do not need to change into that which never encounters disruptions while in this world. All that is necessary is to recognize that since you are a part of All That Is, the Supreme Power of Love, you will always have a reference place. You will develop a growing and deepening rapport with the Most High. You shall know always your power and your safety. The bond that is then created is unlike any other in all existence. It is a continually changing bond, a learning bond. That is the place of your enlightenment, your surrender, your serenity and your light. It is through this that you shall know all that is your purpose in this world.

– Miriam, Isis, Morgana

DIVINE MANIPULATION

Divine manipulating may never entirely stop for humans, but it does not have to get in the way. If contact with the Source is your priority, then in serving that contact you will unravel much and have a reasonably happy life that is extremely rewarding. If you have not noticed, this is not the easiest place to be, so you do not want to keep trying to get everything right. It will not go that far. Just do your business the best way you can and move on. It will get very much more beautiful.

– Merlin

DIVINE MOTHER

There is nobody who is an expression of the Divine Mother who will say they are the only expression of the Divine Mother. The Divine Mother energy expresses through a number of aspects and they all serve exactly the same purpose. Those for whom an aspect of the Divine Mother is their Master cannot see the other aspects and they are not meant to. Almost everybody who is in love with an aspect of the Divine Mother will say, "This is THE Divine Mother in person and this is the only one," because that is how a person feels about their Master. And one cannot feel any other way if that one aspect is their Master.

– Philos

DIVINE RIGHT

Divine Right is not issued, but must be claimed by entities who awaken to it.

– Miriam

EARTH

There could still be a World War III in another sixty to seventy years, but it will not destroy the earth. However, people are averting it more and more because their consciousness is shifting and they are becoming more cooperative rather than competitive. A competitive environment creates winners and losers, and there will always be more losers than winners because the losers marry and create forces against the winners. That kind of war can go on for a very long time. However, it is already becoming more and more inter-cooperative here and if that effort succeeds, then you will never have to see a Third World War.

There is a certain pattern of demise that the world was headed toward because of the great imbalance in nature, the ozone layer and the shifting of the earth on its axis. Things of this kind have been predicted to bring the earth to its end within less than ten years. This is not what is going to happen. The movement to care about the planet has caught on and many people are beginning to be more conscious of the things that create destruction of the planet. This has reversed the trend toward destruction. If people keep the trend that heals the planet, it will be healed instead of destroyed.

The only problem that then will remain is nuclear waste. This must be reversed lest the world will come to an end in about ninety years because the waste shall outlive its containment. This project is already being guided by Spirit and by some who are agencies of Spirit in the world. The solution, which will not be discovered for some time, will have to be how to turn your nuclear waste into non-dangerous forms of energy.

Nuclear waste, which is stored in various places underneath the ocean and the land, shall need to be exhumed and exported off of the planet until a solution is found, for the nuclear waste shall outlive any possible containment. It is likely that waste shall be placed on the moon. There are those who will want to send it into space or into the sun. I have this to tell you, those who visit your world from other worlds shall not allow that.

– Philos

EGO

There are many in this world who appear to be spiritual, but who are simply riding on their ego. Sometimes what appears to be success to another is simply no more than an ego trip. The day shall come when the ego shall have taken them as far as they can go. They will not understand the despair as they hit bottom and find out what they have been riding on has not been the highest truth, but simply an ego trip.

– Miriam, Astarte and Devorah

❖❖❖

Two sides of ego are, "I am better than everyone," or "Everybody is better than I, because I am the worst." Those two sides of ego are exactly the same thing. It is really saying, "I am alone and beyond help."

The ego is thoughts and feelings of separation, which you cannot fight or condemn. How can you condemn a feeling of being separate? If you feel separate, then you must have union.

The ego is innocent. It is not good or bad, but it is what it is. So when you feel separate, notice it. Get close again by first acknowledging what is going on. Second say, "Help me see clearly." Third say, "Give me the strength to follow what I see," which gets attention quickly. Fourth, start looking for the little coincidences.

Some people do not want to do the work that it takes. Sometimes it is hard work to embrace who you are and to heal yourself. Sometimes you would rather blame somebody else or make somebody else responsible. But do you know what kind of karma comes from saying, "I am good and you are bad?" You then must purge the bad in the name of the good.

– Sun Bear

❖❖❖

The hardest part of the path is not receiving powerful awakenings as in meditations or just opening to the Spirit for it to flow in. You can do that most easily. It is not coming to trust, even though that may seem very difficult sometimes. The hardest part is allowing your ego to change, letting yourself become a different person, allowing yourself to leave behind your flawed nature sufficiently so that the flaws do not create tragedies and terrible darkness.

What separates the boys from the men and the girls from the women is the desire to change for the good in the face of the compelling desire for rebellion and fight. That is the hardest part, and it takes effort and work. The tendency is to want to find an easy, softer way, but there is a point where you face extreme effort to choose love. That creates your character, which attends your higher shifting.

It is then that your enemies will begin to come and say, "You have changed greatly. What is different about you?" That is when those whom you have loved most deeply and who have loved you most deeply yet have resisted you, come and say, "You are a different person than I thought." And by that you become humble and start to be able to receive love.

This is also the point where those who were enemies, who wish to remain enemies, whom you have loved, are split from you because they will not accept yet that there has been change. Therefore, they disappear from your life, repelled in resentment and distrust by your very nature. They cannot be in your presence. Or it might happen that they can embrace you and say, "Ah, yes, I love you now. In fact, I always have." There are then no more barriers.

This could also go a third way. They could say, "I must think about this, for this means more to me than I can comprehend. I see that I am not yet made ready for the transition that you have undergone and I must undergo also. You have deeply affected me and my life can never be the same, but for now I must go and ponder this and begin to find my way."

-- Enoch, Philos, Isis, Rapheal and Michael

❖❖❖

Significant resistance is experienced as suffering. To balance resistance and therefore the suffering there is a smashing of the element that you understand in this world as ego or identity. The smashing produces a sense of death, transmutation and transformation. Because there is little understood regarding the teaching of surrender and great primativeness currently in the psyche of humankind regarding the real understanding of love, this smashing is experienced as brutal and difficult. If there were a deeper understanding in the psyche of humankind of the earth, this would be a most elevating, precious, simple and harmonious natural development, a gift. Therefore, those who have made such a journey tend to wish to reach back to those who have yet to make the journey so that their way may be made more simple, easy, safe and free of resentments.

– Domo, Bodhidharma, Ribazar Tarz the eternal and Enoch

❖❖❖

The ego is attached to many paradigms in this world, (physical, nonphysical, psychic and emotional), which are developed and cultivated by humankind. However, your ego is a very odd thing in relation to a higher dimension of existence.

When you seek an entry into a higher dimension, there are certain elements of your ego that function in the lower realm of the higher dimension. At a certain point though your ego is totally and utterly disabled because what sustains it are the paradigms that are created and exist here in this dimension. These paradigms are a part of what your ego feeds upon as it continues to develop and grow. In a higher dimension there is no sustenance and your ego dies totally and completely. There are other dimensions of self that grow in other ways in a higher dimension, but not the ego.

– Yeshua

❖❖❖

When you are about the business of the Source of Existence, there is a tremendous force that drives your life. Sometimes this force is unmanageable to the soul it comes through. Indeed, it is only able to be received at those times when you are in a receptive position, willing to let in the Spirit. Such receiving causes you to lay aside what had previously driven your existence, which is also the Source, but in a smaller, stepped down version of It. Even that tiny version is a formidable power that is far stronger than the intellect.

That tiny version of power is called the personal will. It is driven primarily by instincts to survive, including emotional, physical, sexual, and social. Your personal will is so formidable that no matter what it is that you decide intellectually, if it counters the drives of your personal will, your will eventually wins out. When the intellect is in harmony with your personal will, you collect a strong power around you that forces itself through the world creating your personal intention.

When you walk along a path that is truly a spiritual one, your personal will is submitted to a larger force. At such a time you become distinctly aware of what is termed the ego.

The ego and the will are not the same. The ego is what you identify with as self. It may be in harmony with your personal will to some extent, or totally dissociated from any awareness of your will. The ego, or those beliefs you have about yourself and all the powers contained within those beliefs, may be a constructive or destructive formation of identity. Whatever your ego is, you become aware of it at the time you embark upon a true spiritual path.

The reason you become aware of your ego is that through your attempt to grow spiritually, you become aware that there is something between your spiritual embrace and the place you are now. That something is the ego. Your ego includes all the beliefs you have about yourself and all your desires, whether associated or dissociated from your personal will. Since your will also drives your ego, it is more powerful than your ego. Some may call the will unconscious conditioning. Others mistakenly call the will the super-conscious self. Whatever the label, its condition is basically primitive and fundamental, and it can be skilled and powerful if it is aligned with the ego.

The spiritual life however, is another dimension beyond your personal will and your ego, which can incorporate elements of your ego. The spiritual life totally psychically transforms your will and the fear-based survival drive behind your will to a divine love. As a result you no longer become concerned with yourself and your survival, the drives and the needs of your personality and your ego. Instead, at the higher levels of spirituality, you become more and more concerned only with the expression of the Supreme Love, which has answered your most potent prayers.

Concern with the Supreme Love and how to serve It is often born of great pain, suffering and desperation. The pain eventually becomes the awareness of a dark side for which you grow to be thankful. You find that your dark side allows you to truly embrace the Divine.

For others who do not embrace their dark side, but come to know of their spiritual existence without pain, desperation, suffering and personal turmoil, it is because their soul is already humble. Their ego is not something they have sought to reinforce. They have submitted their personal will to the Divine prior to having the need for their ego to replace the Divine. With those who experience great turmoil, their ego has replaced their connection with the Divine.

As the spiritual life manifests, so that you are in the total embrace of the Supreme Love and all its divinity, this is called an awakening or ascension. For some, this level of ascension is immediate and very sudden. In a moment they are in the embrace of the Divine and their ego and will, in alignment with the Divine, are no longer motivated by fear-driven instincts. They are no longer interested in expanding the needs, desires and plans of their ego. They only seek to express in service to the light, which is where they have found their joy.

For most people however, ascension or awakening is not like that. For most, it is very gradual so that you are revealed things daily that cause you to let go of your understanding and construction of your ego. You gradually replace the fear-based motivation of your will with the Divine Source of Love. The need to embrace the necessary things for the security of your physical existence is replaced by a trust. Your needs for emotional and physical security, for prestige amongst your peers, to sustain your physical existence through sexual relations and the drive for food all become motivated from a serenity that your existence is being fulfilled on every level by the Supreme Divine.

Gradually these places in your being are systematically removed. The fear is removed and replaced with Divine love. Daily, your experience is about allowing this psychic change. This is how you enter the fourth dimension.

– Astarte and Miriam

EMBRACING GOD

Nobody understands the magnitude of what is happening with awakening because what is being done is so immense that the only way it can be done is a miracle. It is not a matter of knowledge, technique or method. You simply look back at some point and ask, "How did I get here?" You will find out you got there a day at a time.

None of those who do it even knew they would get there. They have believed they wanted it but have said, "This is far bigger than anything I can do." There have been many who say, "I know I am going to do it." None of those have made it, not even one, because that is egotistical.

The only way it can be embraced is by recognizing that the embrace is way beyond you and therefore totally dependent each moment on the grace of the Great Spirit. This is what all of those, including me, who have crossed have found in common. Then we turned around and shared that message with those behind us.

Some have listened and some have not. The main ones who have not listened are those who said, "I can do this immediately," or "I will get there someday." They have not made it. The ones who have made it are the ones who have woken up each day and said, "I can do this again today."

– Chief Great White Eagle

EMBRACING THE LIGHT

Those who are embraced by the light shall forever manifest themselves also as ordinary human beings with frailties and faults, even as they are embraced utterly and completely by the light. They come to a place of comfort whereby they no longer fear the Spirit of the Universe. They do not think that the Creator Spirit will force them to suffer and cause them pain in order that they may be purged, purified and embraced by the light. Nor have they become spiritually arrogant thinking that they, by their spiritual practices, are higher and holier than the rest. The Creator does not ask perfection, only willingness, then the rest comes.

– Philos

❖❖❖

Our presence in your dimension shall be intensified for another nineteen or twenty years. During this time many will be gifted in the same fashion as Spirit God has prepared the few in days of old. Those who merit it, who are practiced and devoted shall indeed be those who shall bring in a higher vibration.

After that point, then human beings shall have to reach in the ways they have traditionally had to reach to access Spirit: through great devotion and dedication to service, which have always been practiced by the Masters and Yogis. The ones who have been sincere during this time period shall have the rewards of the gifted.

– Philos

EMOTIONS

Your emotions are a quickly passing reality, which are there and then they go. A feeling is a state of being or a form of knowledge that comes from your intuition, not your intellect. This is an awakened condition that allows you to be in touch with your emotions. A feeling knowing has a broader reach than an intellectual knowing and gets established by getting in touch with your emotions.

– Sun Bear and Chief Great White Eagle

EMPOWERMENT

If everything is inside of your own consciousness and all of your experiences come from your perceptions, then who else can advance, evolve or change those perceptions but you? No one can. So of course it benefits you to see life in such a way as you are empowered.

Mastery is learning how to see yourself in empowered ways more and more. Some would say this means that they can pick and choose the reality they are experiencing. That is exactly right. You see, life is a very good teacher because if you make up a reality that does not work, life will show you fast. So, just go ahead and make up whatever reality you wish to make up as long as it supports you and let yourself enjoy the process. You are not alone here and you are actually much wiser than you realize.

– Motambi Motombi (Mo)

ENEMIES

It is impossible to go to the light without attracting detractors. Thus, you must pray for your enemies. In other words, you must ask Spirit God to guide them as well as you in the way that is highest for them. This is not necessarily in the way that you might think is good for you, but the way that is highest.

It is much more important that an enemy is prayed for than angered over or sought to be manipulated. If you have prayed for them and if there is any openness on their part, they will receive the input. This is presuming that you are content to surrender yourself to the highest light available.

Assuming you have done that job and that you are already in the highest flow, then you are asking for others who are involved with you, particularly enemies and detractors, to also be open to the highest flow that is for the good of all and to the detriment of no one. This is a most important prayer. It cannot be ended simply with one request, but must be used either every day or every single time fear, doubt, anger, rage or any reflection of negative emotion or thought surfaces in your mind regarding such a person. Ask for them to be guided as well as you and you will see the miraculous and the beautiful unfold.

There will be junctures at which you seek to exert the Cosmic Will with your personal intention. While well meaning, your personal intention may not be as well founded as Universal Will. Only surrender shows you who you are at the highest level and how to function there.

From time to time you will see where aspects of your nature that are misdeveloped trigger other people's issues. You can seek to have Spirit help remove these aspects from you, having been made aware of the specific circumstances in which these things arise. Secondly, having asked to have these things lifted, you must be quick and repair what has been done if there is a way to do so.

Where there is nothing that can be done, then ask that the one who is your aggressor be facilitated by Spirit so they may find their higher light and that their light prosper them and you according to the Highest Will. You cannot debate over these things or overly think about them. You must let it go in this manner because if you search deeper than recognizing your contribution to it and seeking to repair it, you are only going deeper into the problem. At that point you must let go by asking that they and you be assisted and go on with other things.

It is your praying for your enemies that frees you from your negative bondage to them. Through praying for them your fears, arrogance or denial becomes apparent. When you cannot resolve with the person directly, the healing then occurs between you and Spirit. The anger, if there is any, then goes toward God who can manage it and receive it. It is dealt with spiritually. That is the most effective place to work with anger after you have done what you can in the physical. This is what brings about the miracle. It is not only because it will change the material circumstances if possible, but because issues that you did not know you had clear up so that beauty and freedom you did not know existed can begin to appear. It is here that your life becomes totally a spiritual event.

There are always places where you, even for the highest good, cannot control events for the highest good. If that were able to be done, you and Spirit would have taken over the world by now. However, because you cannot control other circumstances or people, use your power and connection to God to petition Spirit to help you and others to be open. Spirit will intervene on behalf of the prayerful. If that prayer is for the highest good of the other, this becomes our job. Your job is to ask and ours is to act.

– *Philos*

ENLIGHTENMENT

There are many initiations into enlightenment, many experiences and awakenings of enlightenment until the final stage is reached for every individual and for all of humanity. Each individual can go as quickly or as slowly as needed, which is essential to existing in a state of being that is without a struggle.

– Merlin

❖❖❖

Enlightenment is total appreciation and acceptance of what is going on in your existence right now, wherever you are, while you are also becoming what you are becoming. It is having a sense of peace about now and a sense of peace about the process of life.

– Philos

❖❖❖

To be fully enlightened simply means that you have found reason to love yourself all of the time, as you are right now and are able and willing to fully appreciate each step of your process. However, it does not mean that you shall never encounter a surprise. Enlightenment means simply a kind of flexibility or a willingness to come quickly to appreciate anything that unfolds as an opportunity.

– Philos

❖❖❖

Enlightenment is about a lifting and a freedom from your own inner demands, which is ascension.

– Astarte and Miriam

EVIL

In truth there is no evil in the world. There is only a consciousness dwelling in people that is more enlightened and a consciousness that is not as enlightened. There are choices people make to not allow their consciousness to change, to not allow themselves to grow. They become convinced that where they are is it. That choice is to remain ignorant and that is perhaps the closest thing to an evil.

– Shakyamuni Siddhartha Gautama (The Buddha)

EVOLUTION

The human beings of this world are in a deep engagement with the evolution of their spirit, yet they do not understand the nature of what is unfolding. Those who seek simply with an effort and a willingness to work hard to uncover truth receive pieces of revelation. If there is a commitment to service, love and light, then the various pieces will come together as the people of this world come together. If there is not that commitment, then there will not be a sufficient understanding to bring about the next phase of higher destiny for human beings in this world.

This work that I have just described is no individual's business here upon the planet, but rather is the business of the Lord of All. The participants who do as I have described and are dedicated and persistent shall have a beautiful experience and shall have an honor that is part of their higher destiny.

What happens to you personally as you engage in such an unfolding is not able to be understood from the perspective of the human mind. It is only able to be appreciated by going deeply into the heart. If the heart is pure with an intention and a practice of facing the self, reflecting and sincerely seeking to embrace truth and love, that produces a beautiful experience. This does not mean the heart is perfect and free of all that is human, for within every human being there is a certain imperfection that must be there in order to live from this dimension. Rather pure means, if the human spirit is willing to work for it, there can be great beauty.

This beautiful experience of life requires a certain shedding of what is perceived to be the reality. This is beyond what anyone could ever understand or appreciate save those who go through it. Yet, the entire world must come to appreciate its relevance to their daily lives at some point, though the entire world will never fully understand it at its deepest levels.

– Enoch, Philos, Isis, Raphael and Michael

EVOLUTIONARY LEVELS

All too many people are too busy worrying about their evolutionary level. In the first place, your development and evolution are not graduated in steps one, two, three, four, up through one hundred. Your development is more like six, one, nine, seven, five, thirty-eight. It goes from whatever vibration you are closest to and therefore most easily able to receive and goes in different orders for different people. For each person however, whatever step they are on will be experienced as the next step. The reason why many people see it in levels of advancement is usually because they want to consider themselves in the highest.

– Chief Great White Eagle

EXPANSION

If you want your consciousness to open more just ask, "What do I need to see? What do I need to learn? Show me."

– Sun Bear

⁂

No matter how expansive and beautiful you are, you have to have some realizations about yourself and some sense of who you are. That makes you defined and not infinite. You then become identified with your definition of yourself.

In order to expand you must get outside of your definition of yourself. You do this by seeking that which is greater than you are. Then your own associations and identifications can be relaxed and something new will fall into your awareness from another dimension beyond this one. The more this is your orientation the more that will flow into your awareness, being and activities. You will then find yourself rocketed into another dimension of existence that incorporates this one.

– Merlin

EXTREMES

It is inevitable for everyone who comes to this earth to bounce between feeling 'worse than' or 'greater than'. The nature of the interaction of human affairs forces people to the extremes of one kind or another until that time they go outside of their own resources to inner and higher resources to establish their balance again.

– Philos

FAITH

Faith is not really like a belief. In fact, belief may get in the way of faith sometimes. What you believe or put your hopes or wishes upon may preclude faith from developing. Indeed, beliefs can often not only interrupt a working faith from developing, but can increase the opposite of faith, which is fear or insecurity.

– Chief Great White Eagle, Sun Bear and Yeshua

⁂

It is faith that you function on when you do not believe anymore. It is faith that drives you when everything else is gone.

– Sun Bear

⁂

The true condition of every single human being is that you are a tiny speck and the universe is very huge. That terrible reality is what those who do not embrace their ascension are afraid to face. They create an imaginary world in their mind where they are who they think they are. In order to ascend you must face the terrible fear and cross that border. That is why the Masters pray, "My Creator, you must save me. I am helpless here in this world. You must save me again today."

The Masters have faced this horrible reality and it is here that their faith was developed. It never really existed until that moment. This is where old souls come to believe in God. Before that time they only think they believe in God. They believe as much as they can in God, but they are really believing in themselves, even though they do not realize it.

– Isis and Miriam

❖❖❖

There is little that can be understood of the higher dimensions unless you have a kind of trust. Little trust can occur without the presentation of all that is fearful. Only to the extent that you have a willingness to encounter the most horrifying fears can there be the gift of faith. Faith is not belief, but is the direct result of spiritual experience.

Spiritual experience comes from within your psyche, not as a result of meditation alone, but from all of life's experiences. These peculiar and strange anomalies occur as signs of a higher dimension and it is important to understand how and why this occurs. Unless it is understood to some extent, it cannot be accepted. If it is not accepted there is the denial of the spiritual experience, which is the only way in which you can receive faith.

Some examples of spiritual experiences are strange turns of direction in relationships, peculiar synchronistic events and miracles, shifts in your emotional being, highs and lows of emotional awareness, profound spiritual feeling, visions of light, geometric figures, nothingness and spiritual despair, inspiration and writing, attractions to particular music and states approaching the experience of a psychosis. All of this can produce near insanity for those who experience it. This has been called samadhi and many other names.

To go through such a period for any length of time can be expected. Many times the result of such experience is not understood by the individual nor by the world at large. Historically many visionaries have received music, science, art, metaphysics and spiritual awareness that have been incomprehensible to people of their day. Their work was only later to be grasped or added to by others who came after them.

This consciousness rarely comes to one person, but to many. It is rarely well received and few even notice it. Sometimes this lack of notice is actually to great advantage for those who could receive it. This higher consciousness must flow into the world though for the human beings of this earth to prosper.

Rare and few are those who are able to receive it in humble enough ways that, through the openness of their humility, they are able to touch the souls of others in such a way as to be appreciated and supported by the people and culture of their day. Usually the culture and people will facilitate them in some ways, but also limit them in other ways. These limits will sometimes protect them and at other times frustrate them.

Only with extreme humility, or perhaps better described as openness, can the path be made clear. It is important to understand that there are certain laws of the universe that if found, allow such an individual to find happiness, joy and freedom. This joy, happiness and freedom are directly proportional to allowing the ego or identity to shift.

Identity shifts do not come about in accordance with your intention, but rather they come about in accordance with your ability to understand the necessity of embracing the shift. When there is such an understanding, and thus a willingness to embrace the shift, joy and freedom begin to occur.

– Isis and Miriam

FEAR

The true beginning of letting go of the final fears that hide away in the deep, dark crevices of your black nature and getting into fourth dimensional existence is the realization that nothing matters. This does not mean that nothing is important, but that everything is really all right just the way it is.

– Merlin

❖❖❖

Right now, in this very moment, are you in any sort of suffering due to lack of resource? The only suffering will be in the fear of the lack of something in the future or the past. In the now there will be safety.

There will always be future and past fears to be seen if you wish to look. Once you have acknowledged the future and the past in their fearful aspect, think of how you can acknowledge where there is power, light and love right now. That is what ascension is about.

Right now is where the power is, even the power to create the future in the way that you want. The best way to create the future is to hold the now in self-acceptance, light and love. When fear surfaces acknowledge, "Oh yes, there is the fear again. Let me embrace the truth now."

– Miriam

❖❖❖

We send you messages to support you through your challenges. These messages come through animals, nature, teachers, friends and from the ethers themselves if you are attentive enough and if the motivation is the proper motivation to see into our dimension. The proper motivation is willingness or sincere intention to empty your being of all things that block you from seeing into the realm of the highest dimension of Spirit. That which blocks you is ultimately fear in all of its thousands and thousands of forms. The embrace of love is necessary in all of its most expansive forms without limitation and without hesitation. Thus, love ultimately becomes unconditional and unlimited.

You may encounter many limits within your being and the Spirit of the Universe will reveal them to you. In the presence of those limitations you are humbled for you come to see that you are who you are. The being you are can only embrace so much light at any given time. If you will realize that your purpose is to let go of fear and embrace love, then you can be guided step by step into a dimension of love that is unlimited and unconditional. In that dimension there is no limit on how far you can go and how much love can be embraced. The embrace of love increasingly becomes a life of giving and you become a being full of love.

While you are a fleshy human being, it is nearly impossible to be entirely free of all self-centered or fearful concerns. Yet, if you seek to submit yourself to the power of love, then you shall be lifted through your fears as they occur and great revelations shall bring awakening and surprising gifts that shall lift and hold you in the light.

– Yeshua

❖❖❖

There will be times that you are confronted by what appears to be fear. You might then seek to somehow escape the challenge of handling the difficult things that the fear represents. Realize that all you need to do is to welcome your challenges, embrace them and meet them face to face, while remembering that you are not alone. You will then find these things become resolved.

A great deal of the intensity, beauty and joy that you can experience in your life comes from realizing that challenges are not your enemies, but have hidden gifts of understanding and wisdom that are imparted during such experiences. After a while the fear, which normally would face you by a challenge, will absolutely disappear. All you will see and feel are the gifts.

- Kira

❖❖❖

Every entity needs to learn how to begin and end, how to be born and to die, and how to fully embrace their light without fear. These things need to be learned so you can grow in a gracious, rather than in a traumatic manner.

– Philos

❖❖❖

You must learn to separate fear from reality. Fear is a crime and it is the closest thing to a sin. It is just pure fear, a state of being that you go into when your personal will is out of harmony with the Higher Will. Several things come from that: jealousy, deception, greed, lust, addictions, control, etc. These things are the symptoms of soul wounding.

When you see these symptoms in yourself, you need to stop projecting your problems onto the world and admit that this is your problem. "This is where I lose it and I need the help of Spirit, not with the world outside of me, but with me. This is where I go out of balance with my will and I start trying to manipulate life to satisfy these cravings." The cravings must be handled like any other addiction.

– Sun Bear, Chief, Tall Trees, Two Trees, Sky Walker, Sam Strong Body, Red Sky and many others

❖❖❖

There are two ways you can experience fear: 1) by unnecessarily letting go of what light you do embrace or 2) by going courageously into your darkest places and exploring them.

– Devorah, Helga and Olga, Nemo

❖❖❖

The test you must pass is not a hard one. It is not a physical one and does not take might. It takes one simple thing, remembrance. Remember to see through fear to the truth. First ask, "Who am I and why am I here?" Second ask, "What is going on here? Help me to see clearly and act in the ways that I must." Third, look for the little signs of miracles and little incidents about how it is that Spirit, the universe and your expanded self are helping you arrange this. Fourth, accept that it really does not matter because who you are is greater than that and even though you do not know the truth of that absolutely, you are choosing to become identified with something greater than that which is appearing to attack you.

– Philos

❖❖❖

As an embrace of the true Spirit of the Universe unfolds, there can only be confrontation with the vast unknown. This produces levels of fear such as have never before been faced. Embracing the true Spirit of the Universe also brings an energetic experience that can hold you through the fears.

There are so many concerns that are part of a soul's development, but nothing must exist that is more a priority than carrying the light. As long as this is the priority in your life, then time and time again you shall be lifted up, away and through all other experiences as needed. This will save you. Bringing the message to others who are in need of it causes the angels themselves to collect around you and support and empower you. Never shall you be abandoned.

– Astarte

❖❖❖

Part of the purpose of coming here is to face your darkest, darkest fears and welcome them to be present, no matter how often those dark fears come. No true and lasting faith can exist so long as you are hiding from the fear. You cannot hear the voice of Spirit if you do not want to also be available to hear your darkest dread.

– Miriam, Isis, Quan Yin

FEELINGS

There is a difference between the feelings that are the higher dimensions and emotion. Psychic perception is inside both intuition and emotion, which evolves as you surrender more and more completely to the truth of who you are.

The truth of who you are may be described as something with two realties. One is the God expression that you are that nobody else is. The other reality is the greater self where you are joined with all of the other light beings.

As you evolve into a surrender, into being united in the larger God-self, your own intuition and psychic perceptions take on a different kind of attunement. A different kind of guidance begins to form. You will experience a going back and forth between allowing yourself to be led and events making themselves clear to you. Consciousness then forms within your being. The other aspect is decisions you have to make that are not based upon something absolutely clear from inner and outer signs, but based instead on your own mastery.

The sense of your own mastery comes from seeking to be in a surrendered state. That surrendered state may have to be sought from time to time in intense devotional practices. When it seems that a great decision must be made and you have prayed and meditated trying to get clarity and still it is not absolutely clear, then that is the time to set up a journeying period, a vision quest. This needs to be of your own design or utilizing any existing modality from any spiritual path. Use the time to surrender to Source in your own way.

– Sun Bear, Chief Great White Eagle, Isis, Astarte, Ishtara, Yeshua and Shiva

❖❖❖

You cannot feel something in your heart just because you think it in your mind.

– Sun Bear, Chief Great White Eagle

FEMININE RAY

One of the greatest needs for evolution has to do with the coming in of a feminine ray, which is the aspect human beings call the Mother. This is necessary for in great part women have been denied access to participation in the destiny of the planet except for the raising of children. Marriage, which until recently was for survival, has been arranged for social, cultural and political reasons and rarely for the purpose of love. Women throughout the ages have been little more than a chattel and have been denied access to education and world involvement. Historically this has created a great imbalance in the unfolding of the planet. It has led to a world being ruled by might and force, dominated by the male population who have predominantly avoided emotional and spiritual development. Because of this, as women now come into their power, relationships are being redefined.

– Philos

FIGHTING

Now you go to seminars instead of to master gurus. In these seminars you have breakthroughs in consciousness and you find tremendous exhilaration, knowledge of self and understanding. Your life changes for a while. You then come to believe that if only you could maintain the knowledge and sustain the practices and principles, you could be happy.

I would guess that each and every one of you has tried things like that and at some point you find that you are still a human being. You still must continue to work and your life is still all around you. Your body has not turned into a body of light and you have not floated away.

There are those of you who have maintained an ordered, centered being. You think, "Oh, I now must be by myself because all of those stupid, unenlightened people have vibrations that hurt me and I must stay away from those vibrations. I will only attract those ones to me who are in my vibrations and frequencies that are the higher souls who have come further on the path like me. These other souls, well they will come along sooner or later."

I was like that too. I found out that it separated me from my brothers and sisters and after a while they left me alone. I wondered, "Why am I so alone?" even though I had many people and things around me.

Those practices are not entirely what it is about. There is a beauty that you already have and already are. You must seek that beauty and cultivate it, call it forward. You cannot do it by yourself. You must petition the Divine to help you with it because every day you will need help with it. The fight must stop with everyone and everything. No, you will not do this perfectly, but ultimately this must happen. You will then stop fighting with yourself. The way that you live your life is a very important part of it.

– Siddhartha

❖❖❖

The time will come when all the different kinds of challenges you experience will end. They just finish because the fighting stops. The fight is not with the universe, but is really a fight with your own creation, your own way of looking at things. You cannot win that fight because you are equal to the opponent and the opponent is equal to you. Since everything is you, you win by not fighting, by allowing. Your power then, which you really do not even fully know that you have, ends up focused in the world and starts handling things with so much more energy since there is less fighting going on inside. Watch and you will see this happen today and for the rest of your days so long as you remember this.

– Kira

❖❖❖

Want to fight? I like a good fight. Fighting is a natural part of existence. If you are fighting, you are not suffering. If you are suffering, you are not fighting. A fight is where there are two kinds of awareness or two things that imagine themselves to be different or know themselves to be different thinking they have to understand each other.

I have gotten into fights. That is what led me to love. Love is not thinking that something needs to be the same or different from me. Love, in the way that you might experience it, is letting go of the need for something else to be different or the same. When the need for something to be different is there, sometimes it makes a fight.

The fight is the process by which you come to acceptance. It is a very efficient way to come to acceptance and it is a very good kind of fight to have. If you do not know that, find out about that. In your experience it might translate as having a preference, and if you cannot have your preference, who is hurt?

If you cannot have it the way you want it, let go of having it the way you want it if it is getting in the way of loving, of being in the experience of your love. Sometimes you have to let things be. A fight, a real fight is where you come to terms with that.

Fights for me are pretty much instantaneous. I let things be really quick. I fight with whomever wants to. They will always win. If someone wants to fight, I say, "Okay, you win, what else?"

Sometimes people fight with themselves and they think they are fighting with me. I like those kinds of fights. I can only have those kinds of fights with lovers, the ones who love me. They are the only ones I can fight with. If they do not love me, I cannot fight with them. If they love me, I will fight them and make a quick work of them by saying, "Okay, you win."

There are ways to fight with me that do not do it. When you are hurt and you need love okay, fight with me. If you have ever loved me, you can fight with me and you can win. I am really easy, very easy. "I love you. Help me. Where have you been? Thank you," those work. First remember the ways you love me. Remember what you feel grateful for first.

– God

FORGIVENESS

It is natural when you make mistakes to feel bad. Know that you are not bad and that there is no solution to error. You must eventually and ultimately forgive yourself and then others as you reach toward the ultimate love. That love asks for the ultimate forgiveness of yourself and others. It is your choice whether or not you want to fulfill this forgiveness. The issue is how willing you are to keep going. Keeping going is all about faith, being willing to look at where you are and allowing yourself humbly to move through it.

– Philos

❖❖❖

To accept is forgiveness. It is not necessarily forgiveness the way people might think of it, as though you do a wrong and then you are given forgiveness or make an amend. It is a deeper level of forgiveness that is simply acceptance, which is in fact, letting go.

– Philos

❖❖❖

There is a need to understand that all that is in human form is in some ways flawed. However, all that exists beyond human form also exists within humans. The beauty of the human being is not its perfection, rather its unique expression of love. Perfection can only be the quality of the spirit.

The human dimension needs to be ongoingly incorporated into the Spirit of the Universe so that it might be awakened or reawakened. This continues until all that exists in your nature is compassion or the easy return to compassion. This is no easy task and you will see that even the best and most well-intentioned people will not always remember or know their compassionate nature.

This dimension of the Love Supreme is a great lesson for human beings. For those who are determined to make surrender their top priority, they will remain humble enough to learn that the true way is always about forgiveness of self and others.

– Miriam

❖❖❖

There is a great opportunity to experience breaking through and forgiving yourself. Forgive yourself for not being what you set for yourself to be and forgive yourself for setting that in the first place. This forgiveness needs to be there for only when that truly happens does your judgment of others ends as well as the fear of judgment from others.

– Miriam, Isis, Morgana

FOURTH DIMENSION RELATIONSHIPS

The world is shifting rapidly and is affecting so many people in this highly transitional time. Although the shift is described in many ways by different observers, one way it can be described is shifting from a third-dimensional into a fourth-dimensional phase.

The fourth dimension issue regarding relationships has proven to be quite a challenge. But, I have to say it is going to be a challenge for everyone on this planet no matter what kind of relationship they have. Basically, to have relationship there has to be a fourth-dimensional shift.

Love must transit now from all the forms of possessiveness, ownership and primacy into forgiveness, universal love, unconditional love and cooperative love. This will need to be expanded outwardly from a personal level to a social, cultural and global level or the world will not be able to survive.

This fourth-dimensional shift is not even nearly the final stage in all affairs. In so far as relationships go there will also be other-dimensional shifts, such as the shift from the fourth dimension into the fifth where relationship or union will be androgynous. That means that it shall have lifted to yet another level where union does not even require sexual organs or it may not even require knowledge of the other person. It may not even require a physical body.

Those who make a shift into the fifth-dimensional relationship may not even be able to make the shift as human beings on the earth. It does not need to be done here, but it could be. A sixth-dimensional shift may be for example, no being other than self because the self will have been connected to all Self everywhere.

These different shifts are continually occurring on an individual basis for every entity in their evolutionary path. But, the people of the earth happen to be making the shift collectively because people who come to the earth school come here to make collective consciousness shifts.

One thing that the people of the earth have come here to appreciate together is a fourth-dimensional shift in consciousness that includes relationship. This fourth-dimensional shift has been difficult and has an up side as well as a down side. The up side is that there can be more love, not only between man and woman, but between man and man, woman and woman and groups of people. Children can be raised by organizations, groups or individuals who love to raise children as opposed to simply being raised by their parents who may not necessarily love to raise children.

This restructures and takes love to a new level that will be available, not based upon blood and family ties, but on a more expanded view of love. Wherever there is love that is family, that love will also be experienced on a societal level where more and more groups will come together to support each other in their spiritual, emotional and other kinds of developments. The idea of family will move beyond blood in the fourth-dimensional shifts. This will make new forms of love and support available to many more people in societies and allow for less dysfunction, less loneliness, less pain, quicker healing, and more support. The benefits could be described in a thousand ways and go on and on.

However, the down side of this fourth-dimensional shift is that this is a transitional period and there is no assurance that human beings will make it. There is no assurance that human beings as a people are even ready for it because the third-dimensional state of awareness is still very active and profound. Many people are attached to the positive and negative aspects of it. Their belief in it is strong. They are willing to die for the principles of that, and to keep it the status quo. They are convinced that what the world needs is more of what already exists and are afraid of changing into the next phase, which could take a minimum of sixty years.

This means that most of the life that everybody lives on this planet right now is transitional and without foundation, security or boundaries that are definite. As such, it can be a crazy time with many casualties as the forward movement into the fourth-dimensional shift takes place.

This fourth-dimensional shift has to replace the security that comes from boundaries with unconditional love. Those who have come to know this unconditional and unlimited love will have to become nearly itinerant proponents of it in order for it to be sustained or there will be no anchor for those who wish to go forward into a new day.

All of the life kind goes through these kinds of shifts or becomes extinct. Right now it is the human being's turn to make a shift from the third-dimensional awareness into the fourth. Because the third-dimensional awareness is competitive, greedy, fearful and jealous it creates conflicts that do not allow for a people to survive. In third-dimensional awareness, when the world was a bigger place, conflicts were not dangerous and threatening to the destiny of an entire planet. But, now a more cooperative system must be developed on the universal and personal level.

– Chief Great White Eagle

FOURTH DIMENSION SHIFT

Spirit has come close to this plane giving everybody who wants permission to be just as significant as those few in the past who were the selected ones. That is going to be relatively easy to respond to when Spirit is close to this plane, but when Spirit lifts we will see who is left.

There are literally hundreds of millions right now who are responding, maybe a billion and a half people, but these people are not consistent. It is very haphazard right now and there is very little commitment. Maybe there are a few million people who are committed in their hearts. There may be less than a million who may be committed body, mind and soul. There are even those ones who may get disappointed and quit or take their will back. Those who are really genuine are a handful.

But any one of those billion and a half can potentially be in that handful. We just do not know until we withdraw from this plane and see who has really linked. We are just taking advantage of the fact that we are so close right now, linking everybody who says, "Yes, I am available." We would like it to be everyone on this planet.

Nobody can see what is going to happen to this world after 2010 or 2012. Before this, we could not see past the end of the century. Now our vision is expanded, but the shift is really in the hands of those who absorb the light.

– *Chief Great White Eagle*

❖❖❖

It is an odd transition to go from feeling very powerful and capable in the third dimension to feeling extremely helpless in the fourth dimension. This can be a very confusing matter, but you have only the choice of waiting. As you recognize that your own darker side continues to be the doorway into more light, you can let go because of the darker side.

– *Yeshua*

FREEDOM

If you wish to be able to change with grace, the top priority on your list of values must be freedom, empowerment, love and wisdom. In order to be free you must risk your security and safety. Day by day you must ask yourselves how you can take another step toward self-empowerment. How can you take another gentle step toward love? How can you take another step toward freedom? That is all, just one step at a time.

– *Motambi Motombi (Mo)*

❖❖❖

That which this world would term ego or personal identity may exist at many levels in beings who identify themselves as separated from the Source. These beings may view the Creator as an authority. A being that recognizes itself as a part of Creation experiences a freedom from such beliefs and structures and is indeed beyond the limitations of human beings in the cycles of birth and death. Ultimate freedom is seeking to embrace that which is the truth more completely and being one with the Creator of All.

– *Astarte*

FULFILLMENT

This world is designed to support your growth and knowing. This is not how it has turned out for many of you. Even those who have found themselves in some ways more successful than others have perhaps simply found that they have learned how to successfully negotiate the conventions. Being rewarded by the same, they have found some measure of satisfaction in their equals, but have souls left strangely absent of the fulfillment that they thought would be there.

Successfully negotiating the conventions around you is not the answer to your fulfillment. At some point, in order to embrace that which you are truly here to understand, you must go even further. Many of you will find yourselves holding to those self same conventions, which have in some way supported your survival, even when the voice of that which comes from beyond is beckoning you further still to let go of that entirely and utterly. Such petition does come from the Source of this existence at some point.

To drag your former world into the Kingdom of Heaven is impossible. The Kingdom of Heaven exists within you and requires you at some point to let go of the old paradigm, which by its nature will trap, imprison and limit you. The old paradigm will not offer you the support and the freedom that you imagined it would bring to you.

– Dormor

Emotional fulfillment can only be temporary in terms of any human relationship. The real fulfillment comes from surrendering to God on a daily basis, letting go of where you are caught, asking for guidance and seeking service. If you want fulfillment on an emotional level, then love the people you are near with your whole heart. Treat each person with kindness, love and respect, bringing your frustrations to the Great Spirit.

Your blessings are very powerful. When you say, "Great Spirit, give this person what he or she needs," then turn your thoughts away, you are free. You let Great Spirit handle the person and you go on your way. Then you just watch what happens.

Romance comes from your romance with God, then projects onto everyone else. I promise you this is how it works. One more thing, saving your heart for any other person keeps you from feeling your heart with any present person. While it may seem wise to save your heart, it keeps you from feeling everything that is possible now. When you do not give your heart because someone is not giving you what you want, that is manipulation or conditional love. That is the game that keeps you from finding the 'right' person.

– Sun Bear

GETTING GOD'S ATTENTION

There are two things that get my attention: "I love you," and "Thank you." Do not forget about those things. I know there are lots of other things because helpers tell me all the time. "I love you," and "Thank you," get my attention. Try those first and then complain, it might work.

– God

GIFTS FROM SPIRIT

The Creator gives each person a gift for a specific reason, but the gift never really belongs to that person. You need to do something with the gift. In the best scenario, you do or try to do something that is really beautiful with the gift life after life until you do the right thing with it.

Through learning to use the gift, you go through issue after issue until you are filled with grace. Inside of you it gets smoother and smoother for you, even though the outside world may be filled with challenges. By giving away this gift you get a potent revelation to find the true and real gift inside yourself. Then you are feeling united consistently with the Great Spirit and you will have a very powerful message for the world. All there will be inside of you is light, which will be your treasure and true, real gift.

– Sun Bear

GIVING

The earth is still an infant in terms of numbers of people coming into ascendant awareness. Very few have done it here at this point. The key is giving the light away. That is why we want everyone who has it to give it away. That is the fastest road to your beauty and to make your light stronger. Put yourself in the position to pass the light along again and again. Deliver it to others and help that next person who reaches you. Who knows what they will do with it?

– Chief Great White Eagle, Sun Bear, with Miriam

❖❖❖

There are many stages of lessons in giving and receiving that a human must journey through. When you come to the end of those lessons that appear to be separated into giving or receiving, you shall come to a place that is the still point in which you come to know that the giving and the receiving are all one. So it truly matters not whether your lessons appear to be on the side of giving or receiving. Even though there seem to be some differences they are opposite sides of the same coin. As these energies blend and merge in the union with the Beloved, you shall find that you are both the beloved and the beloved, the giver and the receiver. As such, the giving and the receiving are one.

– Miriam

GIVING UP

After a while you stop making issues with the world. You manage the issues because you put them in the hands of the Supreme within, who keeps guiding you every day. That Supreme Consciousness, which you can access within your being, is an unlimited resource that always has more to show you. It is who you really are, but the only way you can really be it is to give up who you think you are and let go to Its direction. The beauty comes from the fact that the quality of your existence continually becomes simpler and better. That is how you become content and serene. Seeking less and finding more is how it works.

– Yeshua

GOD

You draw God Itself to be aware of you through your devotion, your practices and through raising yourself to the level where you can be seen as an entity by God. Then you must live your life knowing that God Itself has your attention and you have God's attention. You learn how to choose what you want in the sight of God, knowing you are being watched and you are being present to God.

– Miriam, Cassandra and Ishtara

❖❖❖

Many people have a difficult time talking to me. That is why I do not come. Too many wish to put me in the package they wish me to be in. You would like to see me in a grandiose way saying, "Yes, my child, beloved this, beloved that, dear one." I want to come to you closer than that.

– God

❖❖❖

When it is said that God will appear to you it means that you will be acknowledging or recognizing this power demonstrating in your consciousness and in your life more and more. Every time you feel that, acknowledge it. Say, "Thank you." That is one of the things you must know about Source, God is a sucker for love. Any time you have great appreciation for Source, It just wants to give more and more to you.

– *Constance*

❖❖❖

I love you now. I love you forever. I love you in your spirit and I love you in your body. I love you in your soul and I love you in your being. I love you in all parts of yourself. It makes me happy that you love me.

Look for me in many ways and you will be able to receive me more when I come to you directly again and again in personal and impersonal forms. I want you to recognize me any way that I am. You do not need to fear that you will or will not be able to do that. You must remember that I am the Supreme Instructor and I will find ways to teach you. Will you have faith in me in that way? Can you stand me this personal with you?

– *God*

❖❖❖

To approach God, you must first get rid of the God of your understanding from childhood if that is a judging and punishing God. Then you must find another God, the real one. This is the one from whom to seek help. To ask for help you must contact that God. If you do not know how, you will always be brought people who can help you do that. Now, once you have an experience you must pass it on for that opens you up more and more. That is why the key is service. The more you pass it on, the stronger it becomes.

– *Merlin*

❖❖❖

I will come every time you want, not always in the form you are expecting, but I will always come every single time you want.

– *God*

❖❖❖

God must come in a form that you can perceive. It is never in the form that you might expect, but always in a form you can recognize if you are willing.

If your intent is to know your Guides and God then you can. Your Teachers and Guides exist in a realm between worlds, somewhere between this physical dimension and that highest dwelling place. They are tangible enough for you to be able to allow both the wisdom of your super conscious self to take form and raise within your being and the awareness of the God self to come to you from outside who you know yourself to be. This comes from beyond the perimeter of your own awareness. That is why God and Spirit, which are all a part of the same thing as you, must come from outside of your conceptions that you might expand in some way that is recognizable to you.

– *Merlin*

❖❖❖

I have always been here. I never left. It is you who have felt the separation, who needed to pull away from me to explore aspects of your being. You have been crying out for love from a place of deep agony within your soul for many years and you have not heard me. I have been here in the faces and voices of all of those around you, and yet it is you who have not been able to see me. I have received your rage and your anguish, yet it has been you who have needed to receive me. You need to learn the way of the heart.

I am in your everyday life in the most ordinary and mundane way, which is why I speak to you in your own voice. You have to understand that you are an aspect of Me. Be yourself completely. Know that you are worthy. You are Me. If you do not question my worth, then how can you question your worth? You must know who you are. You are love itself. This love is the very fabric of all existence.

– *God*

❖❖❖

The Source is love. When you meditate upon that or are present with that, something happens to your mind. To know God you must know yourself. That self you must know is what is present here with you now.

To know God is different from believing in God. God does not need your belief. You might need your belief. God needs you to know God, to experience God and to know yourself.

You are greater than what you think you are. Your capacity as a human being is unlimited. The God self that is with and within your being right now is thankful to you and is glad for your existence.

– *Merlin*

❖❖❖

The revelation of the name of God shall translate increasingly into a reality that takes place around you until that which is inner and outer are recognized as one and the same. That oneness is the experience of truth that goes on constantly and supports you in every single way. It is important to see that all that is happening around you is for the purpose of increasing your understanding, love, support, service and light.

– *Philos*

❖❖❖

The name of God is "God." The name is not a title. The name of God is a vibration. It is a living force that inspires you to remember and surrender. The name of God will grow in you more and more, and become alive in you. You become one with the name and the name becomes one with you. It is a sacred and ineffable name that is a living presence and it is remembrance.

– *Philos*

❖❖❖

You are centers of energy through which the Divine flows. Some of you have beginning inklings of that and others of you are more fully aware of it. That is what you are doing here in the world; you are experimenting with the density or imagined matter that you call body in order to know that the power of God flows through you.

By the way, matter is imagined and you imagined it. You are continually imagining it and through your imagination you are creating your body all the time. You are taking this imagined construct, which is the easiest for you to believe, to come to know the power of God. That is why you are here in the physical body; this is the level of consciousness at which God can become a reality for you. You are letting the God force intensify in your being until you totally know that it does not take a body to have the God force flow through you. No matter what state or dimension of awareness you are in, you can live in the God consciousness and you can direct it through these very ways.

– *Merlin*

❖❖❖

You are a part of Me and I am a part of you. You are Me and I am you. Do not try to be Me. Do not try to do it. Be yourself and you will know who I am. I will know who you are.

– *God*

❖❖❖

I am not male. You can say Him, Her or It, but none of those is accurate, and I do not like to be called 'It'. There is what you might call a male aspect to power. That is not God. It is a male aspect of power, the ruler of the world, testosterone. That is not my world.

– God

❖❖❖

You are meant to ride the winds of grace, to sail on the beauty of God's light.

– Miriam, Astarte and Devorah

❖❖❖

Am I unlimited? I have not found anything that limits me except one thing, your choice to love or not. That is the one place where I find limitation. I can influence your choice and I will gladly do it if you will let me.

Why should you do it? There is no reason. If you want to find a reason to do it, I will agree with you. If you want to find a reason not to do it, if you want, I will fight with you. If you want help, you have it.

I will not go against your decision to close me out. I will not allow you to close me out without lots of powerful influence to the contrary. You cannot die because you are in me and I do not know the meaning of death. The worst you can do is close me out. Then you might experience dissolution, but you will be born again in my being, so you cannot die.

You can suffer. Do not do that if you can help it. And if you have suffered, I mean it when I say I am sorry. I am sorry for your pain. That does not stop it, I know. I am working on the amends. It is more than what you would ask for. I can promise you that. It might be the best thing that happened to some of you to have been hurt because I like to make the amends. I do not like that you are hurt. The amends will always be bigger than what you would ask for and always different. They have to be if they are going to be bigger.

– God

GOD CONSCIOUSNESS

Humanity is at a particularly exciting time in its unfolding. Many have the opportunity for breakthrough even though the many shall not consistently respond. This breakthrough is indeed significant, for the human beings on this earth are capable of changing or refining the destiny of this entire world.

It is important not only that human beings join their larger universal family, but that they have a spiritual awakening. That is, human beings must aim toward God consciousness. Without God consciousness as the primary requisite, no matter what other kinds of awakenings occur, the human race shall not fulfill the great destiny it is meant to fulfill.

Even though there is a great awakening in terms of the level of consciousness and the rate of growth in comparison to the rate of growth even a thousand years ago the growth is still not yet nearly enough for the true destiny to be fulfilled. It is just enough to get human beings through a time of crisis during a time of great earth changes. Much more must be done if the greater destiny is to be fulfilled.

In order to do this, each person who is awakening to their light must place their desire to serve above all other things. To serve means, you give with love. Giving with love means not sacrificing, but instead giving what you have to give by asking for the assistance of the All That Is, the God and Goddess, as it were.

As you are proceeding forward toward your destiny, it is important that you are alert and sensitive to the manifestations of Spirit in your life. In addition, and far more important, be aware of the love at work in the universe and your love toward the Creator. Then love and peace come and what comes from you is more and more from the love of giving. This is your awakening, and all of Spirit who tends to you is focused on assisting.

Undoubtedly, you have discovered that life so far is not easy. It is not meant to be easy, but instead to be stimulating, challenging and rewarding. This can only come about progressively. First, utterly and entirely accept that you and the Creator are one. The Creator's will and your will become one, not simply because you decide it, but because on a daily basis you recognize the importance of asking for and letting go to this. Find the experience of the Creator that loves, not the experience of Creator that condemns, judges and punishes.

Simply be willing, not even sincere, for sincerity is not most important. Sincerity comes in the next step, which is honesty. Honesty is more than simply being factually accurate and it must be honesty with yourself. You need to be very willing to look at and face every aspect of your being to see what changes must be made, allowing the force of Spirit to facilitate in those changes. Finally, because of willingness and honesty, you become open. Openness is perhaps the most important quality. Openness without willingness and honesty is not openness at all. It is desire for what you need, but not the openness to truth.

This is the path that creates a deeper openness than you have ever known before. It is an openness that brings into your awareness an absolute knowing of rightness, peace and freedom from the sense that life is closing in around you. It is an experience of life supporting you more and more, even though that support does not always mean ease. It is not meant to cause suffering, for even though pain is sometimes necessary suffering is not. Suffering is simply cycling and recycling pain rather than experiencing it, facing it and moving through it.

This kind of healing can be an ecstatic and blissful experience because it creates a shift that most human beings love to experience. That shift is a liberation, a moving through a barrier into your next level. While there will always remain a wonderful sense of challenge, there shall be no suffering and no difficulty, only a willingness to embrace the lessons and the love.

– Sun Bear

❖❖❖

There is nothing reasonable about love because love is an unreasonable, unfathomable power. The action of the God-consciousness is decidedly unreasonable in many, many instances.

Moving from the reasonable to the God-consciousness requires an extraordinary amount of surrender. When I say extraordinary, I do not mean the quality of the surrender, for the quality of the surrender can be even greatly insincere. I mean instead the quantity of surrender, or the number of times you choose to turn your life into the hands of the Guiding Force.

Ultimately faith is developed, faith in the face of everything, no matter what other emotions surface. No matter what circumstances surface, the willingness to faithfully keep going and asking for guidance is the most powerful tool that you can utilize.

– Philos

❖❖❖

It is a gift to be able to experience life at this point, in this dimension. Yet, the intention of the Supreme Creator, whose consciousness dwells in every part and aspect of all existence, is known absolutely by no one. But, all respond to that intention and can find it deep in the core of their being. Those who would seek truth and love with courage and dedication find a most special unfolding, the truest and greatest gift of life.

There are many who find the core intention with such power, potency and profundity that they become completely consumed with God consciousness. Sometimes this occurs to such a degree that such beings are identified by others as God-beings or God-men and are heralded as Avatars and Masters. Their consciousness is filled with God's intention and God's awareness.

Even so, no such being truly is completely aware of the presence and intention of Creator Supreme, even though such consciousness may consume them totally and completely, for if they are in any way human, then they are also human beings as well. And if that anomaly of God consciousness and flawed but beautiful humanity has purpose and intent in this world, that purpose and intent can be beautiful.

– *Yeshua*

GOD'S PERSONALITY

Each entity meets and experiences a Creator with a personality. That personality, whatever it might be for that entity, would be different with a different entity; not because they need it, but because it is like a lover. That is romantic you see. Do you not see how the universe is one big romance? God is like a very incredible artist with a temperament and motivations that are very different from what you might conceptualize. But the Creator, the Source definitely has Its own distinct flair and flavor.

– *Constance*

GRACE

Grace is a very simple thing. It is dispensed, you might say, by that which is at the source of all existence. It does cost something and is dispensed for one and only one price. The price is humility, or shall we say gratitude.

– *Kira*

❖❖❖

When you can remember what there is in your life to feel thankful for, especially at the times when you are the least at peace, that is what brings grace. That which is at the source dispenses grace for those who are grateful. This is the only thing that you need to remember and it is only a question of remembering to remember. This will bring you great, great peace of mind. It will allow you to let go of those things that are effortful and will allow grace to give them to you as a gift.

The only other principle necessary to understand is commitment to your spiritual path. If you can remember thankfulness and commitment when you are in need, you will be surrounded by more and more beauty, growth and joy. These are the keys that bring to you the further fulfillment that you may desire in your existence here.

– *Kira*

GRATITUDE

Gratitude becomes action and that is what keeps you in the light. All of the God consciousness that comes to you comes from trying to give. There are times when you just do not feel it or have it, but remember that your primary purpose is to share the light that is given to you. Pray to Great Spirit to give you the power that you do not have so you can give it away.

Life becomes a constant prayer. If you pray for the light for yourself, you could ask until all the buffalo have died. But when your intention is to give it away, incredible power flows through you. If you want to see and feel this power flow through you, your intention must be to have what interferes lifted, then turn your attention to service. Say, "Great Spirit, give me the energy I need to be this light." This becomes the constant prayer.

The final step in surrender is the giving up of what stands in the way. It may be relentless, antagonizing personal desire gone unfulfilled or people or circumstances that stand in the way. If your prayers are, "Great Spirit, help me with this so that I can get on with your work here," then something greater than you expected is given to you. Nobody on the planet will ever understand that except people who have been through it.

– Chief Great White Eagle, Olga and Helga

GROWTH

Human beings grow so much through thinking and reflecting upon their lives that it is hard to accept that this is not the best way. That is because all of the thinking and reflecting occur through discriminating, judging and moving forward in that manner. When a human being is truly growing, even though they may have utilized techniques of reflection, judgment and choice, growth actually takes place by living the experience, no matter what you have previously assessed.

True growth takes place in the passion of the moment, in the feeling, presence and prescience of the moment. In this state of being, all of your needs are met. As soon as there is an urge in the here and now, there is always an opportunity to fulfill the urge so that no lingering need should remain. This only exists when you have found unconditional and unlimited acceptance or love. In that state, you are continually making progress, taking steps with people, circumstances and the events in your life. Every single one of them is a part of it all and is an element that is vital toward this forward movement into deeper and more expanded levels of your truth.

– Philos

GUIDANCE

It helps not to wait until you have a specific need in order to ask for guidance. If you have a specific need, good. That is one thing and it is better to ask and receive than never to ask at all.

Sometimes what you ask for does not come. What you want may not be what you need. What you want, you may have to learn something about, so what you ask for may not turn out the way you expect. But, the best thing to do is to just start your day with, "Hey, Great Spirit, Guides come here! I want your guidance for this day. Show me again how to go."

It is not because you are stupid, because you are brilliant and beautiful. It is because we are not intended to function independently from each other. We are a cooperative effort. We need you and you need us. That is how it is. When you ask for assistance, things begin to unfold. A time will come when you will be one with the same thing with which we are one. That is our goal, not to create a dependency in you on us, but to link you with the Great Spirit the way we are linked with the Great Spirit.

-- *Sun Bear*

GUIDE POSTS

If I shout, I will get your attention very easily. If I become very quiet, it is harder to hold your attention because it is less sensual. The more sensual it is, the greater your attention.

The planes above the physical operate the same way too. The astral plane is also very vivid and clear enough to hold your attention because it is still sensual. It is where you go when you dream, travel astrally and imagine. You can still have feelings and sensations there, but you shift so quickly from one point of focus to another when you are in that dimension of consciousness because it is less sensual than the physical. This allows you to move very quickly from the future to the past. It is more fluid, more etioplastic.

The planes above the astral become less and less sensual so that you must use more awareness to even feel them. By the time you are aware of the presence of Creator Itself, you must be very sensitive. So you have a few things to go through before you embrace Creator.

Sometimes the Creator comes into more dense dimensions, eventually into the physical dimension. But, maybe God cannot get your attention and needs a Merlin or a Goddess or another as an instrument to get your attention. If you follow the guide posts on the inner dimensions, and that is what Guides are provided for, you will end up where you need to be in the higher states of awareness. Utilize the guide posts that appear.

– Merlin

GUIDES

We are here to help you let go of what you no longer need to hold onto as your identity so that you may come to embrace the larger whole and your larger self. We are here to link you with the Source of All Existence. We are not the Source of All Existence in Its entirety, but are here to help link you to that with which we are deeply linked.

– Merlin

❖❖❖

We have a certain limited power when it comes to working with people. When you seek God, ask for guidance and then do as you think the Creator would do. We are sent to make the result come out in a manner that is beneficial to you.

– Yeshua and Ribazar Tarz

❖❖❖

Each of you has at least two animals amongst your Guides, usually a smaller one and a greater one. When it is time for you to meet them, they introduce themselves. They are companion spirits that desire to be acknowledged on the same level you would acknowledge another person.

- Dormor

❖❖❖

Our nature is one of pure love, of a love essence that is totally invisible. It is totally insignificant and unidentifiable to anyone with pride or ego. They will either think us fools or unimportant and allow us no part of their agenda until they are ready for what we have to bring.

Our dimension has a place in it that is like a physical place. In fact, you could theoretically travel in a rocket ship to where we are. But, you could not exist in the part of our world that is in the physical because your physiology is too dense and you would die.

– Dormor

GUIDING FORCE

The earth has been here without humankind for 99% of the time, because there is an intelligence at work that far outlasts and outlives human linear intelligence. It behooves you to learn that guiding force, the Source of all of that. It is perfectly developed within you now, but you must refine your ability to access it, commune with it and understand it. You must establish the priority of how to respond to it. This might be a different priority than the one you have set up to advance yourself. That later one will not take you as far as you could go.

– Philos

HAPPINESS

What do you imagine it will take for you to feel happy? You know, I have seen many, many spirits come over to this side. The only thing that I have seen when beings have crossed that is important is why they did or did not pursue what was important to them. It is totally immaterial whether or not the pursuit brought an achievement. The only thing that makes their soul sing is that they somehow found enough of the truth to practice it. If they had any other things that were disturbing them, those just disappear like they never existed.

Happiness really has to do with learning how to be satisfied in the knowledge that you are doing what feels right for you. It also has to do with not trying to push away the sadness, upset or conflict. You

must simply allow yourself all of your feelings, not only your joys, but also all of your challenges and all of your pains.

– Kira

✣✣✣

Perhaps you think that if things could be consistent in some way, you could find happiness and security. All you can find like that is temporary happiness and temporary security. If you want to be happy with temporary security that is fine; there is plenty of that. Maybe you should be very happy because there is so much of that. But, it is better if you can find something inside of your own being that you recognize as the Source.

– Motambi Motombi (Mo)

HAVING WHAT YOU WANT

Many of you have found that you are good creators. You get something in your mind, affirm it, visualize it and it will eventually happen. This has been very popular in the 70's, 80's and 90's. You are God and therefore you can have what you want. (Sun Bear laughs.)

Yes, you are God. You are a part of God and yes, you can have what you want, but those two things together seem a little crazy to us. "I am the Great Spirit. Therefore I can have what I want." Understand from our perspective it is, "I am the Great Spirit. I have what I want."

If you do not have what you want and need, you do not have the Great Spirit. You are not the Great Spirit yet. You are not at one with the Great Spirit yet. You may be intrinsically one with the Great Spirit and you may learn much by becoming more aware that you are one with the Great Spirit. But to actualize, not simply realize your oneness with the Great Spirit, there is only one way and that is surrender.

– Sun Bear

HEALING

Compassion or forgiveness is the highest healing for the heart.

– Miriam

❖❖❖

You must develop an intimacy between yourself and Spirit, between yourself and Creator and between yourself and yourself. You can seek out psychics and channels and that might be important, but eventually you must do it yourself to reach your mastery.

Healing has everything to do with hearing the inner voice. The best solution for peering through the veils when you cannot see is to ask, "Is there anything else I need to do? Is there something else I need to see? Is there anything else I might be missing that is important?" If you really receive the answer that comes to you from your own inner awareness, then a certain peace comes. You must refine this practice so that you can receive the subtle whispers that come.

– Philos

HELP

In every day you are going to weigh one thing against another, so in every day you must have the priority to know God, to know the Great Spirit. That contact must be consciously sought and it is not hard. The reason it is not hard is because when you have a hard time there is a very simple solution that is: one word: "HELP!" That help is why we are here.

When you are having a tough time keeping your priorities, you must ask for help. But be careful of asking for help with crazy things like saying, "I really need that stereo! If only I had that stereo, life would be better!" We tend not to answer that as many of you may have found out. The reason we do not answer that is because it is not the right perspective.

How can we respond when you say, "It would really be better if I had that stereo or that partner," when we know it is not that stereo and not that partner? Maybe it would be even better if you just said, "I just want it and I need some help." You do not have to throw in, "Life will be better because of it," because then, if we respond, we are in agreement. We are then saying, "Yes, you are right. It would be better," and it is not true. It is not truth at that point for us.

– Sun Bear

Do not worry so much about the rest of the world, about how to get everything in the world to fall into the proper place, or you will miss the point and you will miss all that divine beauty that will begin to manifest.

–Shakyamuni Siddhartha Gautama (The Buddha)

Asking is saying, "Help," when you need, and "Give me," when you need. This is straight talk, right to the Great Spirit. Great Spirit does not like you to be all airy-fairy. Great Spirit likes straight talk, direct, "Help, give me." Great Spirit experiences, welcomes, feels and embraces this like love.

When you go before Great Spirit in yourself saying, "I am not worthy. I am ignorant and filled with all the impurities of the world," Great Spirit says, "Send them somebody to get them straight. Give me a call when they are straight." You have to go to Great Spirit straight. This is what Merlin means when he says that sometimes the spiritual path begins when you shake your fist at heaven. That other stuff is not humility, but is ego. Humility is not self-depreciation.

– Sun Bear

HONESTY

You are provided with spiritual guidance that comes from within your being if you will devotedly and persistently seek it and are willing to embrace a truth that may exist even beyond your present understanding. If you are willing to embrace that greater truth, you will undoubtedly then have to become honest with yourselves. Sooner or later even those of you who pride yourselves on integrity and honesty may not know the real meaning of being honest with yourself as you face the terror of your own mortality and your own struggles and beliefs.

Having been moved forward to become honest, then you can move to yet another stage, which is openness. When you truly become open, you do not need to know that you know. You do not need to seek that which you know that you do not know. You do not need to fear that which you do not know that you do not know. Your very openness will become attractive, indeed compelling to the Truth of this Existence, who shall have fallen in love with you for your openness.

Then it is no longer a matter of applying your devotion and discipline toward a practice of truth, for you are held firmly in the embrace of that which is loving. Then you are focused upon rather than needing to focus upon and held rather than needing to hold. You are then sustained in a spiritual awakening that is beyond all spiritual experiences.

– Dormor

❖❖❖

A confidence grows from being so self-scrutinizingly honest and so true to the self that you come to see how the universe is working for you.

– Imhotep and Balthazar

HUMILITY

Humility is the willingness to see your own character flaws and the willingness to let them go, standing aside of the difficulties, with the help of the Creator.

– Sun Bear, Chief Great White Eagle

❖❖❖

Something about the nature of power and powerlessness is a lesson in humility. The greatest gifts flow through that context.

– Miriam, Quan Yin and Astarte

IDENTITY

Souls do not even know they exist or hold any integrity until they first recognize themselves as existing. After they have recognized themselves as existing, they are asked to discreate the identity that they have created. This is why you cannot be held totally responsible even for any evils you cause in the world. You must create some sense of identity. Otherwise, you would not know you exist. Then you must give that up to find a truer sense of identity. That is why you cannot be faulted for what you had to create to survive.

– *Yeshua*

❖❖❖

You are not a fixed, linear, sequential identity. You are an identity, who lives on many levels all at once, trained to believe in a linear reality that is making you insane. A certain school of your quantum physicists has begun to discover the very particular and important truth that on the subatomic level, matter responds to the thought of the explorer exploring matter. It is even hard to determine whether or not this subatomic level is matter. I will simply tell you outright, no, it is not matter. There is no matter, only organized energies that people perceive because they agreed that it is some sort of substance, but there is no substance.

Scientists are discovering the truth that consciousness not only moves matter as you perceive it, but also that you are that consciousness that is moving it. You are not only what you perceive yourself to be, but a thorough investigation of something merges you with that thing. As you are studying the thing, you become inseparable from it because of your focus and your intention.

– *Dormor*

ILLNESS

Sometimes there are elements of your consciousness that you cannot manage emotionally or intellectually so they manifest as a dysfunction in some part of your physical body. Your body handles it as energy so that your body can heal it, then your psyche is free. Sometimes though, it works the other way; you heal your psyche and your body is free. So sometimes your body does you a favor by taking on things you cannot manage in your own psyche.

– *Sun Bear*

IMAGINATION

Your imagination is the tool you must use to try to translate the energy you receive. The more imagination you have, the more wise and expansive you can be. You must use your imagination to try to translate the formless into meaningful form for yourself and others. You can always find it by asking, "How do I feel?" It is usually some feeling or emotion blocking the translation, and by getting in touch with what you feel, the message begins to get clear.

I must also say it is not always tough. What starts coming is happiness and excitement until you are receiving it faster than you can keep up with it, until you do not even try any more to keep up with it. You will find it is happening all around you all the time and you come to the highest realization of human existence and ascendant awareness: nothing matters. This is not because nothing is significant or important, but because you have arrived at that place that is so synchronized that you do not care anymore. You are in the trust and know that everything works.

It is not that there is no challenge, but you are wise to challenges. You recognize, "Oh, this is a challenge." You flow into what the challenge is all about and you start to look for these areas of growth. We are looking too and that is why we come through a medium like this. If we did not need to grow ourselves, we would not be here.

– Merlin

❖❖❖

Everything you experience in any dimension comes through your awareness and if it comes through your awareness, you have to image it. There is nothing you can understand without imaging or imagining. You must have a good imagination to visit the realms of understanding. Imagination is your ability to allow yourself to embrace knowing, through whatever imagery is important.

Imagery, by the way, is not always visual. The other senses to your imagery are the senses of feeling, intuition, hearing, smelling and knowing. These are called clairvoyance or clear seeing, clairaudiance or clear hearing, clairgustiance or clear smelling and tasting, clairsentience or clear feeling, and clairprescience or clear knowing. I jokingly refer to these as the Clair Sisters.

These inner perceptions are not really seeing with eyes, hearing with ears, tasting with tongues, smelling with noses, but are the inner representatives of your psychic senses. They are your senses of a plane called the astral.

Each of you translates the sensations in different dimensions of awareness. The easiest sensations to interpret are from dimensions of the astral where there is still sensation, but it is above the physical plane in a realm you call imagination. When you die you will find that out because wherever you go when you think, wherever you spend time in your awareness when you have no body, guess where you will be?

– Merlin

INDIVIDUALITY

There are some who feel that as they embrace more of their spiritual reality that somehow they will lose their unique beauty and individuality. You do not become lost. The part of you that you treasure is always there, always. You find more of your unique beauty and expression and discover what is special about you. It is an experience of embracing more of what you are, not losing that which you wish to keep. It is a gift and it is happening right now with all of you all of the time.

– Merlin

INFINITE

Your journey is infinite, my brothers and sisters, infinite. There is no end.

– Philos

❖❖❖

The universe you live in exists because of an incompleteness within the Source of This Existence, within God. You may say, "Oh, Mo said a terrible thing. How can God be incomplete?" If God were a finished product, God would not be infinite. The moment the infinite finishes is the moment it is no longer infinite.

The Source of This Existence felt a need within Its being to transcend Its nature even further, hence this aspect of existence you live in. Understand that the Source is continually seeking to transcend Its own nature and you, as particles of It, also have that same desire.

– Motambi Motombi (Mo)

❖❖❖

Perfection is an idea human beings made up out of their pain. Because you are in pain you do not want to err anymore or make any mistakes. You conjure up the idea that there is a place of perfection where there is a relief from all of that, where you finally achieve an ultimate goal. But there is no spirit, including the Great Spirit, Wonton Tonkon, that does not transcend its own nature. That makes you infinite, not that you find some static level of perfection. That perfection is not infinite, but instead is stagnation. That which no longer transcends itself is the reverse of infinite.

– Sun Bear

INNER VOICE

There is something that speaks and when it speaks very profoundly, you must listen. It is not just a whispering voice that speaks once or a message that comes, but a whisper that links many other whispers together that you may have been hearing for years.

There is a voice that when it speaks, links many other things together for you. This does not mean you will not have any fear about it. It just means it is right and you must do it. You cannot avoid it and you want to do it, even though it may feel fearful.

The inner voice must speak many times and in many different ways so that the links can get set up for you. Once you have listened to the inner voice many times, have been responding to it for a time and have experience knowing that this voice is right, it gets easier to listen when it speaks. The voice that comes each time then puts a vital piece of the puzzle together and it is immediately clear.

The voice never comes outside of a context for which you have no reference. It is always part of a vision you have always sensed and felt was right for you. That vision may have been formed before you were born here and the answers and pieces of the puzzle must be revealed to you from within.

– Philos

INSECURITY

Spiritual people do not know that it is okay for them to be insecure. They think they need to be free of all insecurity. Because they think that, they cannot show it or admit it when they are insecure, which makes it impossible for them to ask for help.

That insecurity actually means that they have finally arrived at their point of humility. In that moment, if they are willing to let the Spirit of the Universe be a part of their life again in a way that is beyond them, that is how they become like us.

– Dormor and Dr. Tsong

INTEGRITY

You can go completely into your light, but this light must be maintained on a day-to-day basis. After you have cleared your issues in a major way it is up to you to take inventory every day and see if you have done something that may require some insight.

The areas where people get caught are very few. The problems come from natural urges that every human has as a physical being. These will always be issues while in the body, but they can be settled or unsettled. The areas include honesty or dishonesty, selflessness or selfishness, fear and therefore self-seeking or courage, and giving or social needs for acceptance, love, and comfort, either physically/sexually, or acceptance by society.

Everyone seeks to have these places in their being met. If these places have not been addressed, it creates an imbalance. Your will must then assert to assure that you have these things addressed. If these things are not addressed sufficiently, then your will grows very strong and sets something in that area out of balance. This becomes noticeable where the world brings back retaliation upon you. Other people also have those strivings to be loved, accepted and comforted. If you are involved with others where your wills are clashing, this brings resentment and enemies.

If you are certain that you have been absolutely giving, absolutely honest, absolutely serving and that you are not protecting your own position out of a need to have your own needs met, then you are safe. If the way you are getting those things met is through the Spirit of the Universe, who provides those things for you, then you are safe. If you are not certain, then you must ask Spirit to help you in the areas where you may not see clearly. You are then free to do what you see best.

Go into a space in your being where you are naked before the Spirit of the Universe and ask that your motives be guided totally selflessly in service to the truth. If you do not feel safe with that, you need to look at why you do not feel safe with your destiny in the hands of the universe.

If you are willing to look at yourself each day and say, "Today, is there any place I was misleading? Let me correct it. Is there any place I was fearful and self-seeking or insecure?" If these are addressed and healed you will watch miracles take place.

Every day that you are surrendering yourself naked before the Source also ask, "Is there any aspect of my character that is standing in the way of my usefulness to Creator and to other people? If so, please remove it." You can then be the full light that you are.

– Dormor and Dr. Tsong

INTENSIFICATION

Human beings are in a period that in the earth's plane is going on until perhaps the year 2010 or 2012. This period has been intensifying for the last twenty-eight years and shall continue until the years mentioned. The intensification period is the preparation for all of those who are the light bringers. They shall have so much effect upon the planet in their various capacities that we cannot see clearly what shall happen after 2010 or 2012. Very few can see clearly what shall take place in those times for so much shall have shifted. So much is shifting now in a quantum leap as to indeed make that time unpredictable. It is not even known how well the people of this world shall survive this intensification period.

Some have predicted that there will be a diminishing of the earth's population by either war or pestilence. Others have predicted great and even terrible earth changes. Others have predicted a millennium that shall indeed follow such times. But, no one truly can accurately predict what shall take place because the collective consciousness of humankind cannot be gauged as to how much of the light shall be absorbed.

Since this new day is still about a decade away, it cannot be measured in a noticeable way from your own perspective every single day. It cannot be seen what the final destination shall be or even how each day's events do in fact lead toward one vital expression of the purpose of existence. Therefore, ask the Creator for the assistance to be in alignment with Its Higher Will. Ask simply to be taken to the end of each day, one day at a time, so that you can be in harmony as a servant of Its great intent.

These years that I mentioned are a minute speck in the eternal scheme of things, even though on a daily basis it is even harder to recognize how it all shall lead to a great and beautiful unfolding. The scheme of the Creator is in fact eternal. It is beyond not only ten years, but beyond tens of thousands of years, beyond millions of years, beyond billions of years, in fact beyond all time. This means that it is completely unperceivable. If one cannot see clearly how each day's events lead even to a small change that seems great by earth's standards and will manifest within the course of ten years, how much harder then to see a scheme whose length of time extends beyond time itself.

This is the reason for total and absolute surrender. You can never find enough vision or enough rationale to be able in each day to see enough of the scheme to give your intellect reason for reaching and embracing truth. It simply must become accepted as your style and priority. I say these things to reinforce the nature of your journey so that it can continue to be the priority. It is right and good to continue to let go into something that is not only far, far greater than yourself, but also far greater than your understanding or the collective understanding that all of the Spirit realms could comprehend.

The only place where there is any vision at all and therefore some comprehension is through an experience for human beings that is called acceptance. Acceptance is simply recognizing and accepting in your heart that your purpose is the surrender into the expression of service through the Divine. This translates into a certain meaning in life that affects the incidentals in your daily life quite demonstrably.

There is a strong universal influence upon daily life that is in harmony with that higher, broader and very potently expansive purpose. While that expansive purpose can comprehend your existence, your existence is in some ways a tiny part of itself. As such, there is no need for God to comprehend your existence. Instead, God serves only to influence your existence in such a potent and irresistible way that sometimes the events of your daily life may seem quite overwhelming.

This is why it is very important to recognize that everything that takes place in your life is simply an aspect of the Will of the Creator and that which is not understood can then be acknowledged and appreciated. Through that acceptance you rise into awareness where that which formerly overwhelmed can now flow.

For example, a giant wave may crash upon the shore and cause you to be disrupted. When there is a flow or acceptance you ride the giant wave like a surfer who uses the very power of the tide and rushing ocean as the means to arrive at a particular destiny. This analogy applies to much that is going on in existence at this time. Through seeking to find the understandings, lessons and even pleasure in that which is unfolding, you are carried more quickly to the destination.

– *Philos*

INTENTION

If you want to meet God, you must have the intention to meet God and immense dedication because usually you have to clear up a few things first.

– Merlin

❖❖❖

In the beginning love was all that was. Within this love an intention was spawned. The intention gathered such energetic force that it compelled manifestation into space. Manifestation was first energy and then eventually what you now call substance. But, in the beginning this consciousness was all there was, and it always was.
Humans were spawned originally from that same kind of intention and eventually grew to this point where you collectively are now. This point is where you are able to be aware of yourself, aware not only that you exist, but aware also that you too have influence in this universe. This point is also where you are aware, although less aware, that there is influence beyond yourself that seeks contact with you so that you might share more consciously in Its power of love.

– Philos

INVALIDATION

As you seek to be in your highest self, it is important that you do not invalidate the part of yourself that you are leaving behind.

– Miriam, Cassandra, Ishtara

JEALOUSY

Jealousy, in the purest sense of the word, means the desire to hold to what is believed to be owned. It is a fear of letting go.

– Miriam

❖❖❖

Jealousy is where you unnaturally cut yourself off from what you could have with someone. That is a twist that is very hard to see. You become jealous when you are trying to get to a particular place with someone, but for some reason you cut yourself off from them. It is like when there is something you have to do that you will not do and because you will not do it you cut yourselves off and are incomplete. It is when that other person eventually displays their unavailability that you then feel this twist that you have been betrayed when in fact you never gave yourself. In order to feel loved you must stop cutting yourself off and love completely, then the jealousy stops.

What replaces jealousy if you were to be betrayed after you let yourself love completely? It is not rage, but pain, deep grief, deep loss and abject emptiness, which is a different kind of an energy than the jealousy. You may or may not want that person back, but you feel the grief of powerlessness and emptiness, not necessarily jealousy. Quite often, in spite of your love for that person who may have betrayed you, you do not want that person back. You do not try to get that person back because a trust has been broken and you would rather just get over it in many instances, but that is not universally the case.

– Merlin, Chief Great While Eagle, Amatunkwa and Enoch

JUDGMENT

Most of the time you just feel the way you feel and are the way you are. Most of the time everything that is happening really is okay. Now and then there is something like a thief, you might say, that robs you of that experience. That thief is judgment. For no reason at all except purely habit, in the middle of your happiness, all of a sudden you will think, "What if...." Then you think of whatever follows the "what if" that will be your favorite form of displeasure, then there goes your happiness out the window. This has to do with a deep level of deservingness. Somewhere you may not believe that you deserve to be this happy.

Now if you are still thinking that the world is doing it to you or this person is doing it to you, then I cannot speak to you of that because the first step is to take back the projections. The difficulty people have in owning their projections occurs because then they feel it makes them bad. "Oh, look at what I am doing to myself. I am really bad now. Now I am judging." But, when I say own it I mean to realize that it is going on in the realm of your experience and that the other person is not creating it for you. It is you who has those perceptions. It might not be the reality, but it is your experience.

When you notice this thief, this judgment thought, it is not always about yourself. It can be many things. It can be just a feeling that you discover yourself in the middle of and suddenly you notice that your energy is leaving. When that happens, you can assume you are thinking about something that was about your own unworthiness. Just notice and at that moment let an inner prayer go out. "Help me see clearly. Give me the strength to follow what I see."

This is very important because it opens your spirit to more energy. When you say "Help," you have just stopped deciding you are beyond it. When you say, "Give me the strength," you are drawing it in at that very moment. Then just go about your business and look for little coincidences. When you start to see the little coincidences, it is then that you start feeling very lucky and loved.

– Sun Bear

❖❖❖

Judgment includes being judged, judging others and judging yourself. Judgment comes because there is more to embrace about loving yourself totally, no matter what, and finding yourself deserving of love. This includes your own unconditional love for yourself under all circumstances, no matter what goes on outside of you. Thus, you are facing opportunities to love yourself in places where it is hard to love yourself. It is an opportunity to find your union or communion with God.

By simply tuning into your love, which means tuning into who you really are, judgment goes away. The power and love within your being are quite strong and there is nothing wrong with you. The fact that you can recognize that you are judging yourself is simply an opportunity to feel your power and your true self again. It will then become habitual for you to use everything to feel your bliss, to acknowledge when you do not and then to open to feeling it again. This puts you in states of samadhi and satori.

– Philos

❖❖❖

When it becomes more important to you to experience the power of love than to be right, only then and to the extent that you are able to do that, are you able to consistently embrace the upper most dimensions. You come to lose your belief in the rationale that is born of judgment of yourselves and others and learn how to surrender that judgment and embrace your light.

– Philos

KARMA

You are unraveling certain karma, that awful 'k' word. Whether you remember it or not, a lot of what you have done while trying to get control has hurt yourself and others along the way. That has created repercussions that you deal with every single day. The best thing you can do to keep your nose clean and to get some of that to dissolve is to do the Great Work so that you are not creating more disasters.

– Merlin

❖❖❖

Karmas may create action and reaction, but that is not the spirit of God. That is simply the law. The Creator is permissive and does not judge. The law, you would be wise to understand in that action begets reaction.

Be ready to face all that needs to be cleansed and cleared. Be ready and willing to face what needs to be faced. Some days there are great rewards and other days there are amends to be made. These things are opportunities to finally clear with the law until all things are cleared while you are still alive. Then the action/reaction response that some call karma, no longer hurts or pains you. You are then free in yet another way for you have done the work.

– Yeshua

LAWS

We in Spirit have one law whereas you have many laws; you must breathe, eat and get along within society. Our one law is love. We find any way we can to do it. That is what we do and that is why we come here.

– Motambi, Motombi (Mo)

LESSONS

There are always lessons and they have more and more to do with levels of greater appreciation, acceptance, love, ecstasy, fulfillment and happiness. These replace the lessons of survival, suffering, and toxification of the body, mind and spirit.

– Philos

❖❖❖

Whatever you are trying to understand but cannot yet, the universe must create larger and larger demonstrations so that you can appreciate what you need to be able to understand. In part that understanding is why you come into human bodies. This body has an effect of behaving much like a microscope. Small things can be blown up into large proportions so that you can scrutinize closely what needs to be understood.

When experiences become magnified, you must ask, "What am I trying to teach myself here? What is this conspiracy of events trying to get me to understand?" If you come to any kind of an answer that is positive, the lesson can stop. It does not matter that it is the right or the most right answer, but it does matter that the answer is one you perceive as wise, kind and empowering by your own estimation, not by anyone else's estimation. Then, the universe can stop showing you the lesson.

One further thing, to do so is to dwell in the element of your awareness that is without a struggle. The more you are focused in those elements, the more that tends to expand. Then, that is what is created more and more outside of you.

– Philo

LETTING GO

Anything that shuts down an open mind is something that needs to be let go of because a very open mind is needed for spiritual growth. Everything that shuts down an open heart is something that needs to be let go. For example, anger or resentment, even toward God, shuts you down. So, no matter how justifiable, no matter how right, anger and resentments need to be let go. Total forgiveness is part of the nature of love. Total letting go allows your mind and heart to remain open. This is not based upon reason or rationale, but is the nature of that which the humble do. Learning humility as a replacement for the insecurity/pride syndrome is a part of the lesson.

– Miriam, QuanYin and Astarte

LIE

Here is the great lie that will be proffered to you for your acceptance, "I have found everything I have always wanted and you can too." That is the great lie. Behind that great lie is a sales pitch that is never ending and attaches you forever to the one who sells that lie, or the one who sells that lie will disappear and be inaccessible.

Beware of the great lie. It is sold to souls who are in hell for their hearts are vulnerable and needy and the sellers profit by it. Those who are in need may have a burst of excitement or a burst of realization, but sooner or later they are back in the same place again paying for something else that they think they missed. It is a lie from which those other than the buyers profit.

Listen to the hard truth that will also be right there with that same message; love that is unconditional and unlimited is your destination. You are a human being who is full of light and full of imperfections. If you are willing to work hard for the truth, it shall not be easy, but you are vastly rewarded and through that you discover your true radiance. You will see a message like that. Beware the fast and easy. It is a lie.

– Merlin, Chief Great While Eagle, Amatunkwa and Enoch

LIFE

Life is a training about how to enter the most sacred embrace.

– Philos

❖❖❖

There is no dimension of life that is incapable of moving, not health, love, nor relationships because all is fluid. Simply continue to move into the vibration of acceptance, rejecting no part of your inner or outer being, for they are one and the same. All movement, grace and light come through this acceptance.

– Philos

❖❖❖

There is no esoteric practice with super, secret initiations that will enlighten you or will solve the problems of your everyday life. This is because life is like an ocean with waves. You would no more seek to go into this great body of water and command it to follow your dictate any more than you can say to life, "Flow as I say thee must." Yes, you may find a patch of calm whereby the fluttering of your puny arms and legs may temporarily create waves or may quell some small area, but the ocean is still the ocean.

– Philos

❖❖❖

Life has very many interesting twists and turns that you never expect. While there are always some things that you can see, there will always be many more things you do not see in so far as what comes to you in your future. If everything could be completely seen or were to be totally seen before you lived it, there would not be a 'before you lived it.' If everything were totally known, there would be no future anymore, just knowing.

The known is a part of life, but so is that which comes from beyond your knowing. This is the whole reason existence even is, so that you can have opportunity to meet and greet new unknowns. This is why you are here on earth.

The best way to meet and greet new unknowns is with joy. But sometimes, when elements are present that you do not expect, you can perceive something of which to be afraid. At that time you can ask, "What is this gift that presents to me that I did not expect? What hidden beauties are lying in this gift?"

If the greatest part of life comes from beyond that which you do not know that you do not know, then what do you do with what you know? When what you know or what you dream is different from what comes to you from outside of your knowledge, you get very good at living with both things.

– Dr. Tsong

❖❖❖

Some people equate life with handling maintenance, survival and the accouterments, marriage, family and a little service and contribution now and then. These things are wonderful, but they do not take a whole lifetime to master. You do not come here over and over to get the hang of that. It is basic.

The reason you come here is to discover and express something that is a little bit beyond maintenance and survival. You must be open to look for and receive that. If you must go a little bit out of the way of your survival issues to get at something more meaningful and powerful for you, then so be it.

You have come here to do something between you and the inner higher self, to connect into the light of your existence. That will make you rich, wealthy and supported in the truest sense of those values. Yes, sometimes it takes you off a few cliffs and out on a few limbs.

– Philos

❖❖❖

Life is simply the desire to express energetically, in no matter what way and in no matter what plane you live.

– Helga

❖❖❖

Greetings to you my friends, we who come at this time are named Philos. That which we are is a gathering, a collection of particles of awareness that forms an entity named Philos. You as well my friends, are quite similar to that. You too gather to you a collection of particles of awareness that you label self. Each of those particles of awareness that you have become identified with are imbued with certain gifts and certain limitations.

Your life is for the purpose of learning to allow yourself to let go of those particles of awareness that do not now serve your well-being and embrace a more expansive identity or awareness. This is the process of growth, of evolution.

As you become clearer as to what it is you are here for, you become aware of different levels of existence, planes of consciousness and planes of reality. Each of these planes of consciousness and reality are indeed a part of you and you are a part of them.

The more you are able to grasp more empowered elements of awareness and surrender undermining elements of consciousness, you are able to live existences increasingly with lesser degrees of struggle and greater degrees of light. In so doing you are able to know yourself as an unlimited being of spirit having an experience of living in the earth dimension.

– Philos

❖❖❖

When the Creator comes to your door to steal everything, you think is real and gives you the gift of life, you must be prepared to endure and have a firm foundation in the seeking of truth within, recognizing this is all about an inner journey. The outside shall come to mean very little in that you shall find the truest love and shall learn from this plane, therefore eventually leaving it behind.

– Miriam, Isis, QuanYin

LIFE REVIEW

At the time a soul exits the body, never to return to that body again, every detail of life is reviewed. Not only does the soul come to a sense of its own judgment upon the life, but it also sees every opportunity taken and missed. Often the soul is filled with understanding, gratitude and the sense of remembering what was forgotten. If that soul has been humble to a degree, there is a sense of awe at the beauty of it all. If not, one feels mistaken and says, "I did not know. I did not understand," and is filled with an awe-inspiring sense of guilt and of forgiveness, a sense of love and a letting go to the embrace of the Supreme.

This final review is not meant for the end of life. It is meant to be experienced on a daily basis where a soul sees and reflects and again makes a choice to truly live by coming to terms with life for one more day.

– Miriam, Isis, QuanYin

LIGHT

There are a rare few who have in essence seen a light. In all of humanity there are very few who have embraced the light as their purpose. Many embrace it with their words but not with their realization or actualization.

– Philos

LORD

God is that which inspires a devotional ecstasy in people, which is decidedly personal rather than impersonal. Lord is the form God takes that you are more easily able to access in a personal way. Lord and God are the same thing. It is just that the principle you usually call Lord of the Universe is your personalized God.

– Constance

LOSS

To varying degrees, you become a product of the dimension you are in. The Great Spirit ensures your continued growth by removing that which is untrue, leaving you with your true self. This means that the path of awakening and enlightenment is very much a path of losses.

While many people on a spiritual journey are very familiar with those things they have to let go of, such as compensations they want for the wounds of their personality, they are never really aware of the things they will personally be called upon to let go of day by day. No matter how wise they are in self-knowledge, they are always surprised. They can never be forewarned.

Also, what may be mistaken as things going off track or a lack of support is the path of awakening. That is why there is sadness at times on this path because there is a natural grief at letting go and letting go. From the letting go comes a kind of devotional rapport. Sometimes that rapport is interfered with by resentment or anger. The ego fights with God, "You can have this, but you cannot have that!" It is the soul bargaining with stones, not diamonds. The Great Spirit says, "Let me take everything because you do not know what I have in store for you." Every wound, fear, doubt and demon occurs for you until you are truly willing to be shown, to be humble, to say, "I do not know. I need what you can give." This is the journey.

No enlightened soul ever imagines they will have to face letting go of even more. As long as you live in this world there will continually be losses until you can let things come and go, understanding it as love, not torture.

– Sun Bear

LOVE

What brings us here is love. In the presence of love, all other things become unimportant.

– Yeshua

❖❖❖

There are parts of yourself that you have not discovered how to love yet. My angels and Spirits will teach you how to love the parts of yourself. I cannot teach you the things because I am you. They can teach you the things so listen to them. I send them to you to help you.

– God

❖❖❖

There is indeed a need for the people of this dimension to embrace a greater love and another dimension of existence. If not, life for humans will fall in upon itself. Unless there is the kind of shift in consciousness that allows the true soul's nature to be the guide, life shall be a desperate and fearful clutching to survive. This creates such selfish existences, with humans competing against each other until there is little left.

– *Yeshua*

❖❖❖

I do have eternal unconditional love, but I do not have infinite power. I do not have the power to take my love away from you. There is no way you can instruct me how to do that. It is not within my ability. That is something you are able to do because you have never known the kind of love that I have. Once you know this kind of love you will see it is impossible to take this away; once it connects it is impossible ever for it to go away. You are able to give and take away love because you do not know real love, which is always unconditional and unlimited. As you know more and more real forms of love you will see that it is impossible to take it away. This will heal your fears of ever losing love.

– *God*

❖❖❖

Love will not happen simply by surrounding yourself with articles of nurturance, although sometimes that may help. Love is a choice within your consciousness to experience it even when you are faced with the possibility of other choices. This decision is a power that you must exercise until you gain mastery from exercising this choice and until this is the only choice. It is certainly the most magnificent choice. From that place all light and wisdom come. It is that place where beauty and freedom from struggle begin.

– *Philos*

❖❖❖

Sometimes you need the experience of someone outside of you loving you because you never had that particular kind of love for yourself. This can be the best teacher for allowing healing to take place.

– *Sun Bear, Chief Great White Eagle*

❖❖❖

Besides doing what feels important to you, to love is the only other meaningful thing that people have when they cross over to the other side. What matters is how many deeply loving relationships they have allowed themselves to form and how deeply they have let go. This makes people crazy happy when they cross over. If they have nothing else that is what becomes meaningful.

– Sun Bear

❖❖❖

Such incredible joy happens in the finding of as many opportunities as you can to go past those things that upset you. To love will make you ecstatically joyful now, like you are living in heaven. The absence of having that love makes you sad. The fear that comes up about loving somebody, in spite of their faults, keeps you separated, alone and unhappy instead of loving.

It is a miracle when you can remember to forget your self-dislike and love an enemy. When they go into their own creation of negativity and you are just joyfully loving them, they will say, "What's going on here?"

Love changes somebody who has a negative creation they are experiencing within themselves or toward you. They become, in a way, in love with you. It is wonderful to have many people in love with you and yourself in love with many people. I have found that there is nothing of greater value.

– Sun Bear

❖❖❖

I exist in the power that you have begun to know as love. You have to get the love state that comes through your gratefulness and through your choice to love and then I am there. You can have all the talks, all the fights, all the communications you want, but get there.

I cannot help it that I am bigger than you are. If that makes you mad, I am sorry. I do not control you. I do not control your universe. I do not even know what control is and I do not do it. All I do is exist and I exist with power. Power is love. Anything that is not love is not power.

– God

❖❖❖

Know that it is not your aspirations or disciplines that enable you to glean visions and experiences of higher planes of existence. It is rather a willingness to love yourself for no reason, unreasonably, for love must be unreasonable. You must not make yourself deserving of love or give your love to others only when you think they deserve it. This is reasonable and conditional love. All love, including reasonable and conditional love, eventually leads you to become unconditional in love or you lose it. So in a sense you come here to become unreasonable beings.

– Philos

❖❖❖

Everything you have done has brought you here. Everything you do will bring you to the next place. Whatever that next place will be, you will need to let go of something. You will have to let go of this place. You cannot do it wrong, not if you love. If you are not going to love or you do not know what love is, pretend you do and act like you do. I know that is not very popular these days; you are supposed to feel everything. Well feel everything, then act like you know what love is.

I say that because you do know what Love is and you never forget it. You choose away from it, put it out of your mind or cut yourself off, but you do not incidentally or accidentally forget it. Love is a choice. If you love, it is because you chose it. If you do not love, it is because you chose else wise somewhere in your being. What do you do with all of those other feelings? I do not know. Ask the helpers. But whatever else you do, choose Love.

Choose love, even if love seems hard to know and hard to find. Choose to love yourself and others, in that order. And do not forget me. I like to be remembered. I like to be loved and I like to be acknowledged. I like that. I like to be thanked, don't you? I like the same things you like. I wonder why that is?

– God

❖❖❖

I have journeyed a lot of wrong roads to discover the right one. I know that you cannot abuse your spiritual awareness and power unconsciously, incidentally or accidentally. If you cross barriers that you know are absolutely wrong for you, it hurts, it is a struggle and it is hard. If you then consciously give up everything you believe in as good, you become angry, bitter and insane. But, if you open to love, you heal. That is why it is very important to recognize the power of love as a supreme power.

If there is love in your life, whether it is a person, circumstance, art or God, you cannot follow the wrong path. But, if you find yourself shutting down to love in more and more places, that is where you must watch out because you are taking a step into the dark side.

Do not close down to love. Open up to it and all the other confusions that are going on will set themselves right.

– Philos

❖❖❖

For some it is very easy to think that they are fulfilling the purpose of their life because they are making a mark of some kind. Then, if that mark is threatened, it seems as though they are threatened. The truth is that you are living here for love. You are doing this and all that you are doing for love's sake. You need to experience love and you need to give love. You will, in that moment that you are giving and experiencing love, be perfect and healed. This is your reason for existence.

– Philos

❖❖❖

Love is not agreement and love is not support. Love is only held by truth. Sometimes the truth is not in agreement and sometimes the truth is not in support.

– Devorah, Helga and Olga, Nemo

❖❖❖

Love is a power and it gives way to a lot of emotions. But the unconditional love that we speak of is not the emotion love. Love is an empowered state of being.

You love others best when you love yourself, when you empower yourself. You also love others by sharing, by expressing what it is that you love to give. It is simple like that.

– Motambi Motombi (Mo)

❖❖❖

The most potent influence is the power love is. It is creative, and we are one.

– God

❖❖❖

The reason you are here is to experience and give love. You are here to experience a divine expression of life so beautiful that it is impossible to describe. You are here to live in dimensions of beauty and light so numerous as to make it seem that living in the human body is but one tiny part of that entire realm of experience.

– Philos

❖❖❖

You need to choose over and over again to experience love, not removing yourself for any reason from the truth of your being. The time comes when all feelings, emotions and states of consciousness come within the context of love so securely and safely that the entire realm of human and spirit experience can be known in its perfection. Then there is no need to elevate the consciousness any further for it elevates itself simply because it rests permanently in love.

– Philos

❖❖❖

"My Creator, allow me to bring comfort rather than to seek it. Allow me to bring light if there is darkness. Where there is pain, allow me to bring healing. Where there is ignorance, may I bring wisdom. Where there is suffering, may I bring relief. Let me seek not these things for myself, but rather be of the kind that can bring these things when they are needed. It is in so doing that I am free of my own seeking. It is there where I find the light and the fulfillment of my own soul."

This is a peculiar type of feeling or prayer and is not born of self-sacrifice, but rather of an awakening greater than the understanding of the ego. It is born of an awakening of the highest sort of love, for an awakening of this kind understands that love is 100 percent one-sided; one can only give it and cannot demand it of anyone, anything or any circumstance. Such is the nature of love when it is truly contacted at a point beyond the ego, beyond the dream. It is the part of the being that exists in God, Goddess, All That Is and in the vision. For this reason it seems totally beyond you, for that is the nature of the Infinite.

– Miriam, Isis & QuanYin

MASTERS

Many Masters, as they embrace their fullness in totality, put aside their path and their teachings sometimes because they discovered they are not as fully enlightened as they had believed. Some are misguided and others, who recognize they are not on the path, go on faking that they are. Those shall have many, many challenging lessons as they confront their ego and their desperate fraudulence. Others make a choice to recommit themselves more truly, which creates for them a true path and true purpose.

– Philos

❖❖❖

The time must come when every Master stops fighting and just lets themselves be. They feel like they have fought enough their whole life and they say, "No more," on deeper and deeper levels. That surrender is the victory that brings serenity. There have been Masters like Ramakrishna who, despite their ecstasy, were deeply depressed because they carried the fight. He could have even been called a manic-depressive.

– Sun Bear

❖❖❖

The purpose of a Master is to become the focus for people so that their spirituality can focus. Through that focus on the Master they can have a breakthrough into God consciousness.

– Philos

❖❖❖

One day, when you are following your Master, your inner voice will whisper, "Now it is time to go on your own." How do you think your Master became a Master if their inner voice did not tell them, "It is time now?"

When you get that voice, you must listen to it. It takes a great deal of courage to step outside of a familiar paradigm, but there is no spiritual growth without courage, without great courage.

– Philos

❖❖❖

You are all here to embrace your mastery, not your eternal studentship. You are always a student, for any Master worth their salt is always learning, but the time comes when it is important to express some of that. The different forces at work in the universe are meant to stimulate who you really are, then the juices of your own power, creativity, originality and awareness surface. Then they are cultivated, refined and an opportunity to express them arises.

One of the most difficult things for a budding soul is to know when to let go and move on from their earth teachers and shift into a new relationship. If you really need the help of your teachers, they will find a way to you or you to them. An awakened soul who is a gifted facilitator must let the students go and even expect the student to surpass them.

– Philos

❖❖❖

A part of your mastery comes because you are able to see and then choose. If we were to make you do what we thought was right, not only would you never find your mastery, you would increasingly become more and more miserable and disempowered even though you were pointed in the right direction. You would feel, "I cannot do anything without my Guides. I am nothing. They are everything." You would increasingly hate yourself for the nothing that you are and want to dissociate from that. Your life would be miserable, desperate and unhappy.

Many spiritual people find themselves in this situation because of the way they approach God or Spirit. Without meaning to, they end up devoting themselves to a higher power that they say is everything while at the same time saying they are nothing. Thus, they increase the gulf between themselves and God because they have separated themselves. Separation usually leads to despair.

Surrender to God means that you recognize that you too are a part of God. The denial of yourself as a part of God is not surrender to God, but is surrender to the negative ego. The negative ego is never good at any time. The positive ego can get you through from time to time, here and there, now and then, but the true self is always the most valuable to you.

– Philos

❖❖❖

How many techniques have you learned to have spiritual breakthrough and spiritual experience? Many of you have been going to seminars, classes and reading books for years upon years and could probably teach courses at universities on the subject. However, I wonder who seeks or at least takes just one hour each day to use some of those techniques to contact the Great Spirit?

Many of you may say, "Oh, if I had it come automatically, I would do it." But, I wonder who takes the time every day to cultivate their mastery by experience? Some of you have said, "When I have tried to meditate all that happens is my imagination, my mind. I cannot sit. I cannot do this. There is this and there is that and there is the job. I do not have time. I am tired. There are the kids. There is sleeping. There is the boyfriend. There is survival. There are all of these reasons."

Those reasons, they are fine, but most of us in Spirit have heard them all before. We hear it from you when you come over here. You are the ones who say to us, "Why did I not just take the time?" And we sit there and say, "That is what we tried to tell you."

Just take the time. All of these other things do not matter, but it looks like they do from where you are. You may just have to accept that it only looks like all of the other things matter, even though most of you know that they are not that important. That will not stop them from looking important.

– Sun Bear

MEMORY

Memory is not a function of the brain. It is a journey in which your essence goes back to the desired time to again experience something. When you remember, you are letting a part of your essence flow out of this dimension and into the dimension where something is still going on. This can occur since the past, the present and the future are all occurring now. When you lose an experience or a memory, you can journey by sending your consciousness back to where it is still happening, then that presence will come into you now.

– Kira

MERCURY RETROGRADE

Mercury retrograde occurs so that people can deepen the communications that would otherwise remain at the level of superficiality. It helps people to communicate more deeply and that makes things work effectively, otherwise things would remain static.

– Chief Great White Eagle, Sun Bear, with Miriam

MIND

What will you let rent space in your awareness?

– God

❖❖❖

The purpose of a linear mind, if we might label it in that way, is to inform you about what limitations there are. The purpose of your spirit is to inform you how to go beyond the limitations. The only information you can get from your linear thinking is what the limitations are and how you need to protect yourself, which has its importance. But, when you wish to go beyond the linear mind you have to take a leap of faith.

– Philos

❖❖❖

The reason you cannot control the mind is because it is not yours. Nobody's mind is their own. It is bigger than you and you must flow with it because there is only one mind, a cosmic intelligence. Each entity accesses a part of it and learns to journey to certain places within it where they are comfortable. They journey in the same places so often and develop such a relationship and an association with those dimensions that it feels like theirs. Sometimes many people may journey in the same places and they may feel as though they have something to share.

– Dormor

MISTAKES

The reason you think things matter so much is because you think you are in charge. You are not in charge. You think you can make a mistake that will affect your life in some bad way, but you are NOT in charge. Therefore, it is not up to you to make your life work because it already does.

– Sun Bear, Chief, Tall Trees, Two Trees, Sky Walker, Sam Strong Body, Red Sky

❖❖❖

Many make the mistake of not knowing what they want. What they want is confused with things they do not want. They have to throw out what they want just to get rid of what they do not want, then they judge what they do want as unimportant.

I want to give you what you want. Will you take this from me? You must have the courage to know what you want. Do not be afraid to make mistakes or to walk into territory that seems to be dangerous to you. Have faith in me.

– God

❖❖❖

MUTUALLY RESONATING HARMONIUM

We are about a great work in which all who are willing can participate. It is to raise the resonance of this dimension to a functional harmonium of resonance to cause a positive shift in this world.

If people are unable to flow in harmony with their purpose, there will be an increasingly disturbing disharmony in their aura. The feeling becomes intolerable. It creates either a greater density or causes people to shift to a higher vibration in harmony with their purpose.

Anyone seeking to be in harmony needs to lay down their personal desire and find the intention that comes from a deeper place. Sometimes that personal desire is hard to identify because it is so rationalized. From time to time the universe superimposes its own intention over your personal desire if you have asked to be made willing and to have all that stands in the way of your usefulness to the Creator removed. You are thereby changed each day that you dedicate yourself in this way. Your original desire is then replaced by a cosmic intention greater than your personal desire.

Some are often confused about whether their personal desires will be met. Others have the idea that complete surrender will mean the eradication of all personal desires. It does not mean this. Any person who is an instrument of service is also a part of the universe and vibrating at their own specific rate. This must be included in the cosmic intention, but frequently not in the way that you imagine.

Surrender does not mean the giving up of your personal will to a different will, but rather a discovery of what is right from deep within. It is experienced as a revelation, not as a defeat of your personal intention. You experience this revelation as an awakening into a new consciousness, which is experienced from within. It is a breakthrough of understanding or intuition that did not exist until that moment.

The universe does not dictate or even know what will be created until a willing entity with its own vibration surrenders into the vibration of the existing frequency. This creates a mutually resonating harmonium that is an awakening as much to Source as it is to the entity seeking its source. It is in effect a co-creation.

Since the energy of the awakened spirit is so much larger than the singular energy of a human being who is seeking to be embraced, the cosmic energy may seem unaffected by the smaller entity. The Cosmic Self is so sensitive and aware of all dimensions of Its being that it is as equally joyous as that entity that surrenders into it and experiences any awakening. It is the same with teacher and student when there is any awakening, both are moved to a new vibration.

– *Philos*

NATURE OF THE SOUL

The nature of the soul is that its source is God. This does not mean God owns it, but that the soul is a gift. The Supreme receives your love in return as your soul unfolds. The nature of that love is that there is no need or want except to give. The soul will wither if it cannot give of itself. It is necessary for each person to seek a simple way to give love that expresses light.

– *Yeshua*

NEEDS

Many enlightened souls, on the deepest level, fear their Creator with their most precious need. The Creator patiently waits until you are ready to come with your most difficult area. You often have to come again and again as layer after layer is revealed.

– *Miriam, QuanYin, and Astarte*

NEGATIVITY

If you want to suffer for the rest of your life or for the rest of time until you do something differently, then try to avoid negative circumstances. To a certain extent you can avoid negative situations. Things that are overwhelmingly oppressive are usually a good idea to avoid if you are truly overwhelmed by them. But, you cannot truly avoid what you fear. It will follow you around and get closer and closer and appear in more and more places becoming ubiquitous. It becomes more and more insidious and closes in around you until you say, "All right, what do you want?" It might answer, "Oh, nothing really. I just thought I would get your attention."

Negative energy is one of the best teachers because it cannot do anything to you. It is a part of your life force that you have judged in some way that does not serve you. That is all. Eventually, you are going to give up that sort of attachment. That is also a part of what you are doing here, learning how to relinquish judgment and just be human beings.

– *Merlin*

NEXT STEP

What happens around you occurs for one reason; somewhere within it is an opportunity for your next step.

– *Chief Great White Eagle, Sun Bear, with Miriam*

NOW

Because of particular needs that remain within you, there is a possibility you will think that something other than what is present now, needs to be achieved to fully embrace the light. Since right now contains all there is, nothing else is needed to attain that fullness. Right now is where all the power is. There is nothing further that needs to be done except continuously remaining in the now.

For an ascended soul, everything is now. The future no longer disempowers them because that which was the future no longer exists. The future becomes an expanded now.

The same is true with the past. An ascended soul does not see the past in any way that is based upon fear or any disempowering principle. Rather, when looking upon the past they see that which now empowers them totally. They have grown wise in this regard. That wisdom is held in the now.

From time to time you will still have some experiences in your being that respond to outer stimuli that trigger inner remaining wounded places. For ascended souls, wounds become a place that give them understanding or compassion and no longer causes them pain. This occurs because there is a willingness to have faith and trust in what is going on within and without. This faith builds in the ascended soul so that when there is uncertainty or pain their awareness remains expanded rather than contracting. Then, there is growth there too.

Those unhealed places are opportunities to have faith, to be able to see what is later revealed. Do not replace the faith with fear or doubt in the self or self-incrimination of any kind. Bring light to these fearful and dark places and understand them as opportunities to let go, then watch what is revealed. You will see how, in each specific instance, the universe shall take care of you and everybody involved, bringing light to all. You will see that there is nothing that the Supreme Light of Love cannot manage through your light or the light of others. You will become ecstatic.

– Philos

❖❖❖

There is a part of every being that has a difficult time just taking today for today. Because of that you live in tomorrow, which never comes. The effort must be to live in the day. In order to live in the day, you have to truly accept that your life is in the hands of the Great Spirit. If you cannot or have not accepted that fully, then there is an opportunity to embrace that more if you choose.

When you are in the projection of what is not here yet or are waiting for something to come, it means two things: 1) there is a need to accept that your life has indeed been surrendered to Great Spirit, the Spirit who you love and care about and who cares about you, and 2) because Great Spirit cares about you, there is something right today about the way that it is.

When it is beginning not to be okay, it means you are trying to take the control back from the Great Spirit. At that moment that is what the ego is trying to do and that is where the opportunity exists. This is the part that is beyond you, so say, "Take this so that I can live now." Once you are in the now that is where everything is, including getting whole.

– Chief Great White Eagle

❖❖❖

When you are in an experience where you are saying, "Why am I doing this? Why do I even bother being involved in a life where I must contend with these things?" that is what Spirit, your consciousness and the universe are trying to get you to ask and answer. It is a focus that creates being in the now. No matter what conditions that are around you, what can be there when you get up in the morning are great love, energy, excitement and a thrill at the adventure that lies ahead. That same excitement exists if you know who you are and who you are becoming.

– Philos

OLD SOULS

Old souls are wise, sensitive and vulnerable to what goes on upon the earth. However, while the consciousness of humanity is evolving, it is still not to the point yet that true growth is promoted that is very nurturing to the spirit. As a result, the path of fulfillment for those who come into this world will not be from that which is reflected from the world back to them, but rather from their inner or spiritual nature.

– Francesco

❖❖❖

No old soul listens to what they are being told the first time because old souls are very opinionated and strong-minded. They know what they know and hold onto it with tooth and nail until they see there is a better way shown or proven. That is how old souls are, and this is good. Know what you know until you do not know it, or until something else is known.

– Merlin

❖❖❖

There is a journey that all souls make, the journey from not even knowing that you exist, to total consciousness that you exist. In that existence you are in an interplay with all of the higher forces. In order for you to join the forces, which know themselves as eternal, you must also embrace, on every level of your being, the truth that you are eternal.

– Sun Bear

ONENESS WITH SOURCE

The experience of both the known and unknown leaves room for terror. This is why there is the presence of many Spirit beings around you who will hold you as you go across the border from the place where you are into a brighter light. This occurs much in the same way as those who transition at death and who are met by familiar souls to help them across. The purpose of our coming is to help you establish a strong, inseparable link with us, who are dimensions of the Spirit of the Universe, and to the Spirit of the Universe Itself.

It is thus, that when you encounter the vast unknown you will be accompanied by those who have already made the journey. We will quell your fears as you face the terrifying and awe-inspiring experience of facing oneness with the Source while still in a human body in this dimension. The two things at once are so seemingly impossible and so irreconcilably opposed to each other that it requires the presence of entities of unlimited power to hold their connection to you. At that time, it will be extremely unlikely that you will be able to do anything but go for the proverbial ride. You will be unable to do anything yourself at that time except surrender, so you must be held entirely by those who have made the journey. This is experienced time and time again by those undergoing the educational variety of awakening, which are nearly all.

– Astarte

OSMOSING

It is a matter of remaining willing to be aware of your darkness even though you may not always be aware at all times. If you are willing, then there shall be revelation after revelation to the point that it becomes clear how inculcated your design of being has become with the ways of the world as it exists. This can cause a sense of great helplessness and yet, that is what reveals the path of devotion. At that time it is possible for you to submit yourself to a supreme and loving Divine who will offer you simple and humble opportunities to express in ways that truly heal your hurt spirit. This is the osmosing, as it were, into another dimension of existence.

– Yeshua

PAIN

Do not seek to end the pain that occurs because the desire to eradicate pain will hold you back. You need to surrender to Spirit in order to let go and find a value in the experience of your pain.

To accept that there is a value in the pain removes the charge. Intellectually accepting it does not remove the charge from the pain, but embracing it on a heart level does. Acceptance of what is while making progress the best way you are able removes the charge from the pain and brings the ascendant nature.

The ascendant nature is happy with itself and life. The charge, which comes from the judgment of the self, is removed by the fact that you love yourself for your very own process.

– Astarte

Since almost all evolution in the earth plane is gradual, while there is bliss there can also be times of pain in the dimensions of your being that have yet to further ascend. The acceptance or tolerance of that condition is called humility, and resistance to accepting that condition is pride, which stands in the way of serenity.

Everyone who is honest and on the right path will have to face a great agony of the soul, which no one can escape. The path requires that you be you and that is hard to do, but I will tell you how I did it. I had to learn that my own impatience did not mean that I had to do something. I had to learn to live with a part of me unaddressed, with the knowledge that there was something wiser than I that must know and that would answer me. That patience and knowledge does not naturally exist in people and has to get developed.

– Yeshua, Isis and Miriam

When we talk about trust, we do not mean the absence of fear. The trust we talk about is an embrace of fear and has lots of room for being afraid and doubting. That means that when you trust you are also full of doubt and uncertainty and you simply know that it is all right to be uncertain. This is trust and this is faith.

The beauty comes, but not in 100 percent confidence, bliss or ecstasy. Bliss and ecstasy are a danger and a delusion that many use to avoid their fears. The beauty comes in not needing that any more and in allowing yourself to live the highs and the lows. Then the lows do not go as deep and the highs do not need to go as high.

The beauty is not in the intoxication, but is the fact of existence itself, the actual magnificence of the power of love to allow anything. That has been considered by the Creator to be so sweet that it is the most powerful experience in all of infinite existence. So powerful has that been considered to be that the Creator has felt that there needs to be beings able to experience that sweetness along with It.

The Creator has found that in order for beings to experience the sweetness, they must be free also to not experience it, otherwise they are bound by the Creator's demand. If the Creator demanded it, you would not be free, but you would be safe, therefore sometimes there is also pain.

The Creator has found that there is no avoidance of pain. But, there are myriad forms of compensations or amends to the fact that the Creator acted upon existence in such ways that also created pain. The compensation so far outweighs the presence of pain that everyone has to see it to know how beautiful it is. That is what we mean when we say that you will no longer have to fear your fear or pain because it will be embraced by the context of another dimension of experience that makes the pain irrelevant.

– Imhotep and Balthazar

❖❖❖

Miracles are the order of the day when God speaks to you through your pain.

– Merlin

❖❖❖

There are profound levels of pain only able to be touched by those who are embracing what can be called a closure or completion with this dimension. The only way around the deep feeling of this pain is humility. Even so, humility is not a way of avoiding all the levels of the pain because much will still be contacted. Here humility means that you can accept a profound concession, which is the willingness to go to any lengths for the spiritual experience because there is a profound conviction that there really is no other way.

You begin to trust that there may just be something that exists in life that can help you through the doorway. In order to begin to trust that something else exists, the willingness to go to any lengths must be there. Willingness is not the same as strength, power or ability, but is only an open mind. This is not a totally open mind, but a mind with a crack in it and a heart with a crack in it. The crack is love.

Anything like love keeps your heart open, no matter how much pain there is. That crack of love is the openness to the Great Spirit even though it may not seem to be connected to anything resembling your idea or feeling of the Great Spirit. The fact is, it is the same power so that anywhere that love gets a hold, you are safe. And for the sake of love you will try to keep your heart open because you know you need that love.

Ultimately, the truth is really this: a profound concession that all other things are not really working well allows a willingness to go to any lengths for the spiritual experience. That may sound big, but it is a very simple thing that is contingent upon a little tiny bit of trust that comes from tiny bits of evidence that never stops. Sometimes the evidence can be in large abundance and sometimes only in one or two areas of your life to give you something to hold onto. Those little bits of spiritual experience penetrate into your life enough to keep you open, even though there is a part of your being that would like to shut down. The part of you that stays open feels like it hurts to hang onto hopes. The part that would like to shut down feels like it would be a relief to say, "It's all for nothing." In spite of the place that wants to close down, the spiritual experiences reach into you and force you to remain open to a small extent.

Then, from that small, little place you can make a humble decision to work to open the door further, even though you do not have the power to do so. It is truly humbling because there is no power to do it, only a decision that reflects your willingness. When that happens, you get a little bit closer to riding through the pain, which will be over. The pain may recur again another day or it may recur again in that day, but the pain passes. The deep pain, which people are always afraid to feel, keeps them from experiencing the height of the joy that is available, so you have to feel that distrust and pain.

This is a place nobody on earth wants to go. Before they go there, they have a certain measure of courage, enough to say, "I am willing to go to any depths." What has made them willing prior to this point were all of their spiritual experiences.

At some point the tendency is to say, "Were all of those things really real? After all, I thought that I was there and yet here I am in pain again. Maybe all of that was not even real." On the contrary, it took all of that to give them the power to face this. Nobody wants to walk here, they only think they do. Ultimately they all have to and they have no idea the hell they will have to walk in to finally know joy. Only the extremely humble may not have to walk in hell because they are incredibly grateful for so little. Because they are so grateful for nothing, they never know the hell they walk in because they are too busy feeling gratitude.

Those souls are rare and it is hard to come by them. Most of the enlightened teachers hardly come by them and when they do, those souls are teachers to the teachers even though they are not as far along as the teachers. They end up teaching the teachers great lessons, but very rarely do they cross the great teachers' paths.

– Sun Bear, Chief Great White Eagle, Great Bear and Tall Trees

PAST

The truth is that nothing you see is real and nothing you think is real. The only thing that you see and the only thing that you think is the past and references of the past and that is why it is not real.

When you are in eternal time there is total tranquility, and any vision outside of that peace does not exist. The vision includes all that you see that is negative, all that you see that is positive and all that you see that is neutral. It is all a projection, a hallucination until it is seen through a tranquil eye. This happens by having learned trust, by having all that exists undone so that you are able to see only the will of God, which is one with your will.

– Miriam

PATH

When people begin to become spiritually aware and touch into spiritual experiences, the first response to these experiences is, "I simply want to do whatever it is the Creator has for me to do." The Creator then says, "First you must become empowered to discover and do what it is your soul desires."

As a part of the path of discovery it becomes necessary to become very empowered and to come to sense that in fact, you are an entity with unlimited potential. As an entity with unlimited potential there needs to be a willingness to tap that unlimited potential, express it, demonstrate it and express your mastery to some extent.

At some point there is a shift that begins to take place because you can often encounter many personal challenges, including the inner desire to create or manipulate everything. This desire makes some people crazy. At that point it is time to begin to let go. It is also at that point that the Source again appears in many forms and in many different circumstances and says, "All right, now is time to learn what you originally asked for." You begin to ask again, "What is my destiny? What is it that I am here for?" Then the Creator says, "Now do you want what I have to give you?"

– Kira

❖❖❖

You have found your path when something has begun to speak to your spirit and you have begun to listen. Maybe it speaks to you in the form of an angst, like a pain that is in your chest or your gut, and it calls and beckons to you for something more, something higher. This is sometimes the most torturous experience, but it is a calling.

– Shakyamuni Siddhartha Gautama (the Buddha)

❖❖❖

This sickness is in every human being and has many permutations and forms. It gets a hold of all species and people at some point in time, giving them the opportunity to face it and rise above it, but this takes time.

Humans did not get this way right away, but this came through many lifetimes and will take a while to get better. The craziness of perfection will come back again and again and you must be prepared to treat it by turning it over as much as is needed. Do not seek to become cured, seeking instead to know truth and to be in your highest ability. There is nothing wrong with that.

Instinctually, you will think making mistakes means the end of your existence because that is what you have been taught and what lifekind has been taught. But, there is a higher wisdom beyond the perfection seeking. You need to have room for forgiveness. This is the only way that you can know that you are lovable. If you recognize that forgiveness is a great part of unconditional love, then and only then can you understand why you are loved. If you think you must be flawless, you will think that you cannot be loved.

Those who realize that they can be loved with all their flaws allow themselves to be loved in this way. Otherwise, you will look for flawless beings or for beings who you believe have achieved a certain high state and you will not see the God in all. You will never find the one who has achieved that high state without also seeking and finding many flaws in them. This separates you from the very love you want.

This is the result of the kind of thinking that does not have room for true forgiveness and this paradigm must be relinquished. It is this kind of standard that creates so much delusion and false teaching. What is needed is to embrace what is in fact true teaching, which has room for forgiveness, love and the embrace of the unconditional and unlimited love without the need of perfection.

There will be many false teachings that gather much popularity in this world because they play to the ego. People feel good about the achievement of perfection, which creates a kind of spiritual fascism, a kind of spiritual separatism between those who have done so and those who have not. Unfortunately, this has happened with most of the spiritual movements on this planet, but the time has come to end it.

– Miriam, Isis, Morgana

PERSONAL DESIRES

Personal needs will be fulfilled in ways that appear to be miraculous by letting go of what is called the collective consciousness. Your needs are not able to be grasped by setting and attaining goals and objectives, rather they are met by surrendering to the altruistic or expansive need and watching the personal needs be fulfilled therefrom.

The prayer associated with this needs to be expressed whenever you notice a fear manifesting as disappointment when there has been something you have expected to come that has not. The prayer is very simple, "Let the Cosmic Will be done and let me be a part of that. Let me embrace that as what is right for me." Any fear will then show itself to be present and can be released or surrendered.

The fear that you will not be met by the Supreme will be revealed again and again to offer you the opportunity to surrender into the light. You will discover the greater beauty of the light revealing Itself to you. Its desire for you is greater than any other desire you could have conceptualized for yourself.

It is in this way that a human being, in its ascendant nature, has the opportunity to experience its version of what the Creator Itself experiences again and again, which is Its ability to eternally transcend Its own nature. The human translation of that transcendence is the letting go of personal desire again and again to find how universal desire and the surrender to it will reveal something greater.

– Astarte, Isis, Ishtar, Ishtara, An, Anya and Miriam

PERSONAL POWER

As people surrender, they let go of some of the aspects of their nature, which are vital survival modalities, that have been cultivated over many years. Letting go of great pieces of the self also means letting go of your accumulated personal power, which is a part of the surrender. There is not a way you can do this incorrectly and leave anything out. What is required of you is so simple, if not easy, to make it impossible to be misunderstood. All that is needed is willingness and your ability or inability to let go is totally immaterial.

What comes before willingness is recognition that you have reached as far as you can go by utilizing the paradigm of your old resource. Willingness therefore includes a kind of grieving or saying good-bye to something. You come to a point that you deeply concede that there is not a way to go on in the same vein anymore. You may not even feel certain how to go on, but there is a sense of freedom, hope and even expectancy that you can finally put down the fight.

Surprisingly, it is very simple to pick up the fight again. I myself have picked up the fight over and over again. It is often creeping and insidious, but I have found the solution to this to be a daily review of my being in which I look over my day and ask, "Where might I have done better? How might I have better expressed the will of the Supreme Love as I understand it?"

Willingness is further manifested in a very simple way that can be described in four words, "Thy will be done." It is as simple as a request that the love of the Supreme Will is what you express. This prostration or surrender is followed by going forward as you believe the loving Spirit would have you do. The time comes when there is no longer a sense of battle in any way from what formerly seemed to be your fear driven concerns.

This is a simple dimensional shift that requires no exaggerated or graduated levels of effort. The shift requires only a simple recognition that you wish to embrace a dimension where there is no longer a fight. The aspects of your being that tussle and struggle are somehow comforted by a love that seems to understand, which becomes most available through your intention to serve the consciousness of love.

– Yeshua and Ribazar Tarz

PHYSICAL NATURES

So long as you manifest a physical body, you are vulnerable to the physical natures. The physical natures are not enemies, but rather empowering dimensions of your being. They are not good or bad. It just depends on how you use them.

– Yeshua

POINT OF NO RETURN

When you have had enough spiritual experiences, you will come to a point of no return. From that point forward you cannot go backward because you have realized so much. From that point or any point forward your awakening could be complete. Some awakenings happen slowly and some happen quickly, but all happen when you go forward in a painstaking manner with dedication. As this happens you are then embraced until there is a complete surrender into the light.

– Philos

POWER

You search for power or influence in order to gain some control over your environment. Most of the life forms on this planet are in this phase, from one degree or another to try to conquer the environment. It is a part of the natural urge of consciousness to be in harmony, but control is not necessarily harmony. Nevertheless, the impulse is to try to have some influence and harmony with the environment.

When you go to the higher dimensions and receive guidance, it raises many issues. How do I know from where the guidance is coming? Is it from me, my ego or Spirit? These are issues of not having fully understood yet how to let your will be in harmony with expanded will and this is why you must take inner journeys. You must come to where we live and we can show you how to be in harmony with the expanded will. This is what we are expert in showing you.

– Dormor

❖❖❖

You are trying to embrace power because you do not feel powerful enough to manage your existence. The power that you might think that you are trying to embrace is actually a gift of Spirit. It enables you to function better in your existence so that there is less of a struggle. The power you are actually trying to embrace is the power of so much love in your being that you feel healed, supported and able to work your existence effectively with gentleness rather than force or struggle. There is no point to existence save that love. Love is the power that nurtures and gives meaning to every dimension.

– Philos

❖❖❖

When you accept yourself fully, with both the greatness and simplicity of what you are, that is true spiritual power.

– Chief Great White Eagle and Sun Bear

❖❖❖

Do you realize that the universe was created to confront discontent? There is a part of the human soul that has experienced great pain and is tired of that experience. It is a part that wishes for a state of perfection in which to rest and be in heaven forever. But that is a place of stagnation and is a false path that assures you will always experience pain.

If you realize you are always going to be surprised with opportunities to let go, when this occurs you can get excited. You see it as the very opportunity you needed to get higher. In other words, because you see your frustration, you then have the opportunity to go higher right then and there. Your might and power come from seeing where you can let go and choosing to let go. Power comes from there. Then nothing has power over you and that is when you really get high.

– Miriam

PRAYER

Some of you may have heard an inner voice but not yet found the courage to follow it. Some of you may be in the midst of responding to your inner voice. You must remember prayer, which is you talking to God, and meditation, which is God talking to you. With enough of these dialogues you start to get the point and your awareness becomes refined beyond logic.

– Philos

❖❖❖

The only thing to pray is how to be active in giving, in helping someone else. Get out of yourself and give some light. Ask that what is in you be worked with by the Source. The Source is an incomprehensible inner resource that is always there and must be sought. It is never found if you do not seek it when you need it. Seek it when you need it and it will never fail you. The answers to everything you could ever encounter are in what we have said and are already inside of you.

– Dormor and Dr. Tsong

❖❖❖

The world looks very real and must sometimes. We know because we have all searched for the same comforts in this world. We were all brought to our knees over and over and over again. Actually, when I prayed I stopped falling to my knees and I went right onto my face! My prayers were done flat out because that is how I feel before my Great Spirit. The Great Spirit will pick you up every single day.

– Chief Great White Eagle

❖❖❖

Unless a petition or prayer is clearly and directly stated inwardly or outwardly, all we have is our best assessment from our perspective of what it is you are asking.

– Philos

❖❖❖

All that goes on within you also reflects what is going on in the world. As you feel, you may presume that is also the pain of the world. Your cry to the Divine is how the world cries to the Divine. Your prayers are really the prayers that need to come forward from the people of this world. The part that feels unanswered in you is how the world at large feels distanced from the Divine. As you reach to and find the light, you will also be able to help others reach and find in that way also.

– Yeshua and Milarepa

PRIDE

Pride means an idea or picture of who you think you should be. The ascension, in the moment of recognition of that, is a letting go of that idea and accepting yourself now. What your spirit needs to do is to deeply concede that it is all right to be who you are and to let that be revealed to you, which the ego fights.

– Sun Bear

❖❖❖

The fastest way to contact and know God consciousness and to surrender is to seek to leave behind the aspect of your ego that is cultivated through an idea you hold of yourself and the culture holds of you. This idea is called pride and the pride is smashed over and over again where God is sought.

Those who do not seek to hold their pride intact will eventually manifest the deepest aloneness imaginable. Through that aloneness they shall find God consciousness. The aloneness will not be eternal, not even a great length of time. As most awakenings are gradual, the aloneness will occur over and over again in shades of deepening union with the Creator. This process continues and that which is termed the pride becomes meaningless. At that point you have done most of the work, for without pride you are able to follow the will of the Creator.

– Yeshua

❖❖❖

Initially the pride is there for survival because there is no one there in the way that you need them to be there. As a result, you have to shut down certain dimensions of your being in order to be there for yourself. For those who are in their ascendant nature, the Great Spirit comes in and does a sophisticated form of cosmic judo on that way of survival. It is replaced by support from the Great Spirit that manifests in the form of people, circumstances, causes, places and conditions. In the place of your own strengths based upon pride, there develops an inner security because you recognize how loved and supported you are.

– Sun Bear, Chief Great White Eagle and Great Bear

PRIORITIES

Again and again your priority needs to be your character and spiritual principles over comfort. These things are not the natural human urges, for the natural urge is comfort.

– Miriam and Astarte

PROBLEMS

The older a soul becomes the more complicated it is for them to try to work out their problems. What creates a problem after lifetimes of existence becomes so complex that it is almost impossible to disentangle on your own. Serious problems must be left to be addressed on a spiritual or altruistic plane.

Do so by seeking a conscious contact with the inner power of love that is deep down within yourself. Refine that contact with the power of love and ask that power to help you see clearly how to proceed. That is a conscious contact from which comes the working out of concerns on the spiritual plane. Therefore, asking for help brings a step-by-step process that addresses many aspects of the problem.

– Yeshua and Ribazar Tarz

PROGRESS

All who would seek to utterly and entirely embrace the light will still have within them the ability and the possibility of experiencing the darkness. In the same way, all who are in the darkness have the ability and possibility of utterly knowing the light. Until all human beings are able to embrace the light, then all human beings must also, of necessity embrace the darkness, whether or not they are aware that this is indeed so.

It is for this reason that those who are on their path of light must hold within them the knowledge that there is only progress and never perfection. The progress that is made is dependent entirely on their willingness, honesty and openness. If these things are in alignment, then a soul can always have access to and be a vehicle for that which is most brilliant in all of existence. It is only getting to the point of true openness that makes it possible.

– Yeshua

PROJECTION

If you own everything as a part of you, then God can help you. That is when you can receive the energy of the Great Spirit intertwining Itself with you, creating a total psychic transformation in your personality. It is like the layers of an onion being peeled off. For some it is very quick as they are not here to serve, but are here doing something else. For others it is a more gradual process.

Those going through it gradually are often given gifts along the way that the quick ones do not get. More important, those going through it gradually need the familiarity with all the steps because their experience then becomes THE tool by which they are able to affect and save many others. That is part of how your experiences will become of value.

– Sun Bear and Chief Great White Eagle

❖❖❖

Everything in your consciousness, since you are identified with it and are relating with it, is really just an aspect of yourself. No matter what you think is outside of you, all you can really see and experience is you. Therefore, what is outside of you is really just projections or creations that are aspects of you.

When you experience an animosity toward someone, you are really experiencing some aspect of your own animosity toward yourself. The person toward whom you feel an animosity then becomes immaterial. What you need to do is a little trick to love that person even though there are things you do not like about them. Give them the honor and the privilege of your love.

– Kira

❖❖❖

Externals are simply projections of your own consciousness that you imagine are outside of you. Since it really truly is you that you see, to accept everything is to love and appreciate yourself. Through total and complete appreciation, unconditional and unlimited love, you fulfill the requirement for this plane and are then enabled to break through to a level of greater awareness.

– Philos

PROTECTION

It is important that Masters in no way speak against, condemn nor criticize other Avatars or Masters in any manner. The universe does not take lightly to that. If it is that you are an Avatar, there are further steps for you to embrace. The universe would not have it that you are threatened because you are a part of the universe, a protected entity upon a particular mission that requires that you be sustained.

There are those who speak against Avatars and it might even be said that the universe takes revenge against them. It is not that there is a karmic response for them being bad, just that Avatars are so one with the universe that the universe has to support them. If you go against that which the universe supports, you come up against a formidable force. Thus, when you sense a light in someone, support it unconditionally because that support will raise you further and will reveal to you who you are.

– Philos

PSYCHIC TRANSFORMATION

Those who have forged the way have only been able to carry the flag, as it were, a bit further into the territory of the evolved human being. Most have had to set down the flag only slightly further than the last ones who had made it to that point. Each one clears the way a little bit more for those who would come behind them entering into a new territory, a new frequency of human consciousness.

No soul passes through these points with graciousness and ease. The level of frequency of tests, no one has passed easily and it reflects a true psychic transformation because you are no longer the being that you were at one time. You become a different being, leaving behind the being you were. The new being that you become may reflect many of the elements of your former being, yet you are no longer the same being. In essence, you die and are born again, a process that happens over and over again in one form or another until you manifest your ascendant self.

It is for this reason that there has been so remarkably few who have chosen to continue the journey onward. They have chosen some other level of existence at those points in time rather than embrace the onward movement.

– Jhenrhett Turonok

PURITY

To be a pure soul in this world is very hard because the world will not help you be pure. For your heart to stay pure or at least to be willing to be pure, you must be honest and open. Honesty is like purity to God.

– Chief Great White Eagle

❖❖❖

To see your greatness and your smallness is living in the right size. This greatness and smallness are sometimes so hard on the Masters, yet they keep staying pure. They do not hang up their frock, instead staying and rededicate themselves again and again. The solution is that they keep serving because they want to be closer to the heart of God.

– Chief Great White Eagle

PURPOSE

The purpose for which you are here is growth and that growth brings many beautiful experiences of learning and revelation. Through the revelations you find yourself more and more a part of the Spirit of the Universe, which flows through you, healing your wounds and awakening great beauty and power. This occurs to the point of ecstasy. Ecstasy can simply be gratitude whenever another human being reaches out to connect with you, an agent through which Spirit flows.

– Chief Great White Eagle and Sun Bear

QUESTIONS

You are not here to seek answers, but to ask questions. You will find many solutions and come to many understandings, but you are not here to accumulate theories of existence and to understand all of the metaphysical principles of life. You are here to grasp those aspects of it that are meaningful to you. You are not here to study until you know all of the answers, but rather to learn how to be comfortable and be at peace with questions that are unanswered. Only if you are at peace with a paradox can you know truth.

If you have no room in your being to have questions that have no answers, then you will put answers where none belong. As such, you will make up your own truth and design your own karma from which you must then break away and transcend. If you are the kind of an entity who realizes that ascension, consciousness and awakening mean that your awareness is curious, inquisitive and alert, then you will gain understanding.

Your journey is infinite, my brothers and sisters, infinite. There is no end. No matter how many answers you receive there shall always be more questions. You shall quickly learn the meaning of the saying, "The more you know the less you know." Or perhaps better said, the more you come to understand, the more you are aware that there is even more to understand.

If your joy is based upon understanding everything, then hear me and change it to being based upon learning how to appreciate the moment you are living in right now. Learn to love yourselves in this moment no matter what, for no reason whatsoever. No matter how much further you imagine there is to go, no matter how far you have come, decide and choose to be in the consciousness of love again and again because love is a choice.

– Philos

READINESS

Readiness means the willingness to let yourself be shifted by the Supreme Divine away from the habits and conditions of third dimensional values. This shifting is the redesigning of your psychic being into the dimension of the higher self by the hand of the Supreme Divine Itself.

Aspiration will never bring about this shifting. Simply, readiness means being willing to allow the shift to happen, being honest with yourself about where your darkness lies and leaving other people to contend with their darkness, even they may have hurt you. Ask for your own darkness to be lifted, forget the other's part and ask the Spirit to free you from your part. This process lifts you away from your darkness and the darkness in others and you get freed from the trap of the darkness attracting darkness, which recycles itself over and over. In this process you are changed and serenity increasingly becomes the order of the day, accompanied by the fulfillment of all of your emotional, spiritual, social and physical needs as a result of the Divine.

– Astarte and Miriam

REALITY

The limits of what you term reality must be challenged in order to experience what exists beyond those limits. The way that you expand your awareness is to be totally aware of what you perceive, not avoiding things that seem to have the label of imagination, mind, conception or any of that, while just being totally present with who and what you are.

– Merlin

❖❖❖

All of your experiences are real, but when you have a spiritual experience you shift a little bit into an extra-dimensional kind of state. This extra-dimensional state is a state other than the normal state of being that you label reality where you usually spend your time. Every place that you do not label reality or do not spend a great deal of time can fade away like a dream. That is why people can have very powerful and profound breakthroughs emotionally or spiritually, but when they go back to their normal frame of reference it seems like a dream.

– Philos

❖❖❖

When you seek to embrace the reality of life and existence there is no singular perspective or set of media through which perspective comes that fully conveys truth. The one expression of truth in its totality is available by becoming totally open to embracing the power of love, which is unconditional and unlimited. The best that perspective can offer is to act as a doorway to enter the totality of your union in the Divine.

The divinity experience is very rare for human beings in this world. When life experiences reveal challenges that are beyond your ability to understand, for most people it seems as though the challenges are like reality crashing in upon the illusion of love rather than the truth of love embracing the illusion of the challenge. Until that is totally turned about, all other perceptions than love seems like a challenge to the reality of love rather than an opportunity to allow the reality of love to embrace that challenge.

– Philos

❖❖❖

Embrace your oneness with truth on every level, spiritual, mental, emotional and physical, until there is no resistance. There must be a conscious and continual choosing of this truth. It is then that you will experience the revelation of who you are and what the universe is and you will know you are one. You will be completely free of all forms of delusion or stuckness, which includes the illusion that somehow life, people, spirit, the earth and God Itself can somehow turn on you and betray you. Instead, when you are so one with truth, all will be continually perfect in the sense that you can accept it and see yourself continually embracing light and truth.

– Philos

❖❖❖

The world you are in is very much like a dream. Even the ongoing things in the world that seem to demand your involvements are only a dream. Every part of your physical human nature is equipped to magnify your human experience so that it seems like reality. It must seem like reality in order for you to study and understand it. To wake up from that dream you need to utterly let go of it, recognizing that it is only a dream.

Parts of the dream may seem like they are really a part of your higher purpose because like all dreams, there are premonitions of what is there and what is to come. With all of these things going on in the dream, it is very easy to think that it is the unfolding of your destiny. When that dream gets cut away there are a huge confusion and bewilderment. The bewilderment is the actual shifting beyond the dimension of the dream and is a shift in planes of consciousness. The shift is a leaving behind of former dimensions of planes and paradigms, which is in fact an ascension experience.

It does not end here however. Beyond bewilderment you can no longer construct a picture of any plan, structure or ambition in which you will have any confidence. Instead, if you remain true to your journey, your heart will truly seek submission into the Source. The Source becomes your love and from that, an intimacy and true trust develop with the light. The trust represents another ascendant reality that existed beyond the previous one. It is the leaving behind of the physical and psychic support that opens you to that which is truly new.

– Chief Great White Eagle

REALM OF SPIRIT

As far as the world is concerned, the realm of Spirit is a wispy and ephemeral form, which is a flexible, adaptable and subtle yet brilliant consciousness. This realm of subtle wisps is a powerful dimension. All light and wisdom comes from this place, which is of the highest in those dimensions.

– Yeshua and Ribazar Tarz

RELATIONSHIP

You cannot find a good relationship that you can control because control is not love. Love is unconditional and unlimited, which means it is without reason and without proportion. Love is about letting go of what matters because the demand begins to be not worth it. Instead you say, "I would rather love you than fight with you." Love becomes more important than holding onto what you wanted. That extension solicits love of the same kind in return, which becomes less and less conditional. The more that conditions creep in, the more painful the relationship becomes. Ultimately, you must let go entirely.

– Merlin

❖❖❖

The desire to walk together is important, but it does not manifest the outcome. If it is meant to be, the desire will be there to walk with a person and it must be an intense desire. Of those who present, there are those whose path could be an interference to yours and those who are in harmony. Those who are an advantage to your journey may be an advantage for now, but may become an interference later or vice versa. Thus, you must ask if the way you are involved today is advantageous or not. If today it is harmonious, let it be so. If it is not, then let it be made harmonious. If it cannot be made to be, then let it go. That is the truth of a higher existence.

– Yeshua

❖❖❖

A true holy, sacred relationship is one that is able to continue the love with the building and breaking down of bridges. Or perhaps it has no bridges at all and both beings experience a union of love that has no barriers. Whatever it might be, the love becomes more important than the illusion of some sort of construct that somebody has in their mind to make themselves feel safe and secure.

People think that security is the purpose of relationships. While relationships do give you some security sometimes, and some safety and some healing, the purpose of a relationship is for you to go far beyond these things. Your soul requires that you find your truth in God. If your truth is in God and you experience God in your relationship, then you can get your security in the God in your relationship. Certainly the relationship cannot replace God for you. God must be in the relationship and God must be wherever that is for you. You cannot use a relationship as your God. That means you cannot make the relationship your priority because God must be the priority.

Many people try to make a relationship work by changing themselves again and again. They then resentfully break up years later, full of hatred for each other because they tried to make themselves what the other one wanted or the other one tried to make them into who they wanted. This is so ridiculous when you can just go ahead and love each other totally as you are now without trying to make each other into anything. This does not mean it is going to be the relationship that you want because it will be the relationship that it is. The realization is, "We are going to have to love each other the way we are whether or not it meets our conditions, or not love each other at all."

– Devorah, Helga and Olga, Nemo

❖❖❖

There is a mistaken impression that some have that you must perfect yourself before the love of your life can come. If you perfect yourself and have nothing to do with another love, then you are not perfecting yourself, you are creating a sophisticated strategy of loneliness. What will inevitably happen is that your strategy will become so sophisticated that no one can penetrate it. Well, the truth is that love prepares you for love.

– Merlin, Chief Great While Eagle, Amatunkwa and Enoch

❖❖❖

To hold and remain true to spiritual principles in relationship is to create sacred relationship. The most important spiritual principles to base relationships on are: 1) those near to you simply have the desire to be one with Spirit; 2) those who are the nearest must have the ability to be devoted to your life and well-being and that you be devoted to theirs; and 3) be dedicated to self-reflection.

In order to have sacred relationship be willing to admit fear-based motivation accompanied by action to set things right. Be willing to have a conscious experience of the Divine, the deepening and perfecting of that experience and sufficient spiritual awakening. When these things are present, your experience is full of the power of the message of truth with which you seek to touch the others who comprise your spiritual family.

– Yeshua

❖❖❖

Old souls, in case you had not noticed, do not have easy relationships. They are very particular, fussy and persnickety wanting what they want, when they want it and they want it yesterday. If an old soul cannot get it yesterday, they are convinced that there is something terribly wrong with them or the whole system. Old souls are very self-centered because by the time they have been in this world a very long time their soul really wants to get down to business and get on with it.

The quest for the soul mate becomes a very compelling urge and desire. The conniptions and manipulations that an old soul goes through trying to work that soul mate out creates more pain, struggle and suffering sometimes than it is all worth. They look for the right one who must have all the right qualities in place and then wrangle with each other to serve each other's needs, to come to agreements and to make contracts. Then the relationship does not work and they correct it, doing this and that. Before you know it some children pop out here and there and the old soul has to support the children. The children get into trouble and the old soul feels they have to help them. Then the children have children, and when it is time to go the old soul does not want to go because they feel they are still needed. They then have to come back again and they think they never should have had children in the first place because they hurt the children. The old soul vows to do things better in the next life and then they get hungry for another soul mate. Before you know it they are in a life with ten or twelve soul mates and they cannot figure it out.

Just do the service! There will be plenty of love along the way, I promise you, but if you try to make it happen, oh, you will make so much entanglement.

– Merlin

❖❖❖

Wanting a person in your life does not get in the way of the person coming, but wanting them forever does get in the way. Even though you can be with a person forever, all the things that contribute to you wanting someone to be with forever come from insecurity and that keeps the forever person away. That very desire blocks you from seeing that the person is your forever person. That very intent causes you to check for things to resolve your insecurities that do not need to be checked for because that person does not need to resolve your insecurities. You need to resolve your insecurities and you will never find the person to resolve them for you. So one person after the other can come and go without your ever knowing if they are the right person. The thing to have a care about is if you want that permanent person you must be willing to love deeply whomever you love deeply in the now.

– Dr. Tsong

❖❖❖

Relationships of the future shall be cultivated healthfully between two men or two women raising children, group marriages or serial style relationships with no permanent partner throughout one's life. There shall be groups exclusively dedicated to children comprising people who are more prepared to support life and raise children than those presently doing the job. Because of a great change in the way love and relationships are carried out, this transitional period over the next sixty to eighty years will tax the mind, emotion and spirit of all humankind as they grow into embracing a consciousness that truly supports life.

– Philos

❖❖❖

Relationships are very beautiful experiences. If you want the kind of relationship that you feel is truly fulfilling, it must have many, many aspects to it other than what you had expected.

– Dr. Tsong

❖❖❖

If you are really in the search of love, spirituality and growth, not in the philosophy of it, but in the true experience, then find somebody to love who lets you love them and whom you can love completely. Find someone who is mature and intelligent enough to be able to interact with you, communicate with you and with whom you can engage. Right there you will find the love of your life. That is the truth as I understand it.

– Merlin, Chief Great While Eagle, Amatunkwa and Enoch

REPRIEVE

When there was pain that I did not understand I knew that the trouble was I, not the world, not the external circumstances, not the Father. I knew there were parts within myself that I needed to yield in order to embrace this unnamable and unlimited resource that required something of me to hear Its whispering voice. My awakening to this and the acceptance of all parts of myself was my true ascension. From this realization day forward I was free, happy and truly joyous. There were still trials from time to time and life was still as it was for everyone else. There were good days and bad days in my life and sometimes I wished my family would disappear, and sometimes I was happy with them.

The thing that never happened for me anymore was the deepest part of the pain. I learned to find acceptance for the parts of myself that could never be perfect and as such, I found serenity. Every single day was then a good one in my mind, not based upon achievement, nor the knowledge that every day is good, but because I truly and deeply appreciated this unnamable resource with which I had become one. It was and is my friend and my teacher to whom I do surrender even in my mergence with It. I am never alone. I found that my happiness was in giving away everything I had and learning to love. I no longer sought validation or anything other than this unnamable one and I gave away everything that I had come to understand.

My surrender and enlightenment were based on a kind of spiritual reprieve brought to me depending on my daily spiritual condition. This condition was always kept high by keeping the search and the finding of that Source as my priority and giving away what I had to give.

By facing the real, true issues of the shadow self as the source of your problems and by facing the light as the solution, then you too may be granted your ascension on the basis of your daily spiritual condition. In each day you may be granted a reprieve from that aspect of the self that is the shadow self. It masquerades as real, but is really the aspect of your being that is created by living in a wounded world and believing in sickened principles. You need to balance between the glorious kingdom and living here in this world. You must balance between the two dimensions otherwise you become too distant, not identifying with the people of this world. Acceptance of this brings ascension; the recognition through seeking and finding and ultimately letting go with total abandon to that resource that is then no longer untapped. The inner resource is tapped at the point when you totally surrender to It.

All who seek It shall gradually or quickly find absolute surrender in It, but all will find It. Each finds It in their own way, depending on their ability to be willing, open and honest. Willingness to acknowledge the shadow self and surrender it, increases by asking how you can become the servant to that indescribable power, which is extremely tolerant. This unnamable, untapped resource is thought by so many to be very demanding, and in some ways that can be said to be true, but It is truly not demanding. It is truly permissive. It is so permissive that It will allow many to go the wrong way, as I did.

For those who seek to surrender to It, It is extremely regarding. Those who seek It and ask for change may become more and more filled with It since It is infinite and goes on forever. Then in each and every day, with each new circumstance and life experience, you may be granted this reprieve and embrace until such time as you are in a total surrender and in your ascendant nature. The qualities of this are a joy and a total freedom.

There are those who in this world in whom you shall see these qualities, which are the unmistakable marks of God. They shall not be perfect as some of them will have tempers and others may have various quirks. They will be great or unnoticed people, but they shall have the mark of God, which are joy and freedom. They will express beauty and lightness and they will not be bound.

– Yeshua

REWARDS

There is no servant of the light who has not, because of their love and compassion, taken a route, from time to time, that causes them to work with some of the energies of the planet and the people in the world. By what they undergo, they thus transmute karma and challenge for many. This has caused some pain for the light bringers in this world, and the only thing that God can then do is to see to it that the light bringers are compensated. The compensation shall indeed be in many forms that are miraculous.

– Philos

RIGHT/WRONG

In perfectionism you are still looking for a right and a wrong as if you will be given a present when right and punished when wrong. The very thing that needs to be extricated, the very paradigm that creates problems is the need to be right and the fear of being wrong. The feelings you have of fear must be turned over to God. Let go of this fear into God and know that you must do this whenever you need, not once and for all, but again and again.

– Miriam, Isis, Morgana

❖❖❖

No person enjoys letting go of old ideas, beliefs and philosophies upon which their life had formerly been based. Most people want it proven that they are right and that anything they had believed in will be proven true. Everyone wishes to hold themselves out as special and above and beyond because they fear that they are 'less than'. They experience tremendous resistance in becoming a 'part of' even though they want to be one with everything.

Nevertheless, the time does come when you allow yourself to become one with all. In that oneness you find the safety and beauty of the light. That which is then revealed is greater than anything that could have been revealed in any other way.

– *Yeshua*

SAFETY

Do you wish to go on in the safety of what you know or take a risk in surrender to God as you know God within your being? Will you allow the Creator to design your path for you through life lessons? You will feel an absolute desire to recoil into the safety of the known, being convinced that is right? You may do that if you so choose. I am not here to convince you of the rightness of what I say, but simply to share with you what I have done that has brought me into this union. Only you can decide that you are willing or able to trust. When you are ready inside of your being, do it, which is the telling that the Creator understands.

– *Miriam, Isis, Morgana*

SALVATION

Time and time again souls who have found the embrace of the Supreme have found their salvation in both nurture, which is compassion extended toward them, and in a gift of awakening by losing themselves in the Great Work. In this surrender, over and over again the negative aspect of the self is lost and the brilliant aspect of the self is found. It is in this process that the light of the Spirit begins to shine so brightly with grace that the soul is lifted in the heights of the brilliant light.

– *Astarte, Isis, Ishtar, Ishtara, An, Anya, Miriam*

SAMADHI/SATORI

Samadhi is the experience of being in an elongated period of bliss. Samadhi is the Japanese word and satori is the Indian word. Mastery is repeatedly experiencing your bliss, which simply becomes habit.

– *Philos*

SEARCHING

Love yourself completely, unconditionally, all the time, no matter what. Remember, there is nothing you have to perfect, achieve or do because you are already the state that is most natural, most wise and most evolved. That perfection already exists and it is something you awaken to, discover and find.

Finding the perfection is not something you need to look for because it is so much easier than that. In fact, those of you who search for it may become professional seekers because it is never found by searching, but by feeling and by becoming aware. It is found by being present with all that is right now. Searching takes away from it and it is so much easier to just be present because then there is nothing you have to do. Remember that you are not broken and you do not need to be fixed.

– *Merlin*

SECURITY

In your need to be physically secure you must not steal or be greedy. Even though you have been wounded or have never been given what you believe you have needed in order to feel secure physically at some junctures in your life, you must not allow the nature that wants and wants and wants to control you. Wanting will cause you to become needy and greedy and you will start to justify things, small things. Those small things will create karmas in your consciousness and they will block you. You will start to think in ways as though that part of you is who you really are.

You have a need, an instinct to be physically secure, which is given by the Source of this Existence so you can survive, but at what point will you feel secure? How much work, how much time, how much can be consumed, how much control, how much domination, how far do you want to manipulate in order to feel you are secure? With whom do you want to make agreements about your security and what kind of agreements do you want to make so that you can feel secure? Will you beat your soul mate over their head because they do not make enough money so that you can feel secure and thus chase your soul mate away from you? What about emotional security, what are your demands for that? What about your acknowledgment by your peers, such as "I want to be recognized as important. I want to have a meaningful impact on the world." Everyone has an instinct for that, but how far will you go? What will you compromise?

You must go some place else other than those demands. You must look at yourself honestly because those demands are getting in the way of your communication. If those things run your nature, you must be honest and see where they are running your nature. That is where you must let the light in to help you. There is where you must say, "This is where I need help. This is my illness, my wound, my disease. Help me here in these places." You must recognize this truth because the world, people, circumstances and situations will only go so far.

– Siddhartha

❖❖❖

One of the great illusions is to chase security because you think you are not secure. If you focus upon that insecurity, then it will expand and no matter how much security you seek, you will never feel as though you are secure enough. Besides, you must pay a price for your security. The cost is your freedom because you end up imprisoning yourselves.

– Motambi Motombi (Mo)

SEEKING

You must seek yourself at the source as well as seeking to understand that which is beyond yourself. As organisms and as spirits you are designed to do just that, but without persistent and devoted seeking it cannot be done.

– Miriam

SEEKING CONTROL

Older souls usually find themselves in some kind of service work. At some point some of them even find themselves tired of doing the service work or resistant to it even though they are doing the very thing for which they came. The resistance is because older souls are sometimes secretly seeking control over their environment and therefore they often have a great deal of resistance. When they are actually offering the thing they are here for, they find themselves getting free time and time again and the freedom never goes away. Tiredness comes from secretly looking inside for that control that will give the old soul the way to be free forever. They do not yet really understand that their freedom comes from passing on the light.

– Merlin

SELF-HONESTY

The Great Spirit will do anything for you, regardless of your motivation, if you will examine your motivation and be open for a change. Change is not even necessary, just the openness to change. No matter how flawed, you then walk in the light when you are open. The Great Spirit wants to do everything for you and you then rest more and more in the hands of the Great Spirit.

The Great Spirit wants you to work at honesty and the willingness to shift and wants to do the rest of the work for you. In the eyes of Great Spirit the only way It can demonstrate Its love to you is to give you everything It has. The only way you can receive what Great Spirit wants to give you is if you are self-examining and honest. The reason the Great Spirit wants to give everything is that the Great Spirit always had everything. It wants to share that experience with every entity who is open. What you have to do to get open is what life is all about.

Right where you are you can feel the love because it can come in. Because the love is given to you, it can be given away. You do not have to be free of impure motives, just willing to surrender them. You then end up with gifts of serenity, peace and plenty of outer rewards that you know you will never have to struggle to get. The gifts then just keep coming.

– Chief Great White Eagle and Sun Bear

SELF-KNOWLEDGE

Self-knowledge does not always change the way that you feel and spiritual awakening lies outside of what you know. Oftentimes terror of losing that which you already have precedes this awakening.

– Sun Bear, Chief Great White Eagle

SELF-RESPONSIBILITY

Some people tend to take self-responsibility as a moral judgment of their goodness or badness, creating a big problem for themselves. They are confusing self-blame with self-responsibility.

The only way out of this dilemma is God consciousness. Any other consciousness, including perfection or trying even harder to do it right, does not work. When you encounter this inevitable habit that is keeping you from God, you must own the habit as a part of you that you want lifted. In fact, want EVERYTHING lifted!

– Sun Bear and Chief Great White Eagle

SELF-REVIEW

Do not see past issues that you have cleared as issues that are permanently gone because it does not work that way. If that is your perspective, you will be vulnerable to future impediments and blocks. Be regularly self-reviewing. As you do, the light of Spirit will not only receive you, but will also dwell in you and facilitate you further along your way. A gentle vigil needs to be kept, for humans are not perfect beings. They must enter the Spirit world where there is power and there is light by continually reviewing the self again and again.

– *Chief Great White Eagle*

SELF-SACRIFICE

There is confusion in your era between giving that is self-sacrifice and true giving. As a result of this confusion in the group consensus, every awakened being must face this issue and sort it out.

There is a collective idea that it is unhealthy to give of yourself as a solution to your pain. There are also many who are caught in the disease of too much giving, therefore avoiding their lessons and development and thereby hurting themselves. In every single instance where there is this sickness, the motive behind the over giving was to get something for the self and it was never true giving in the first place. The over giving was really a desire to manipulate an outcome, which is in fact the true disease.

The giving of which we are speaking is the salvation of the enlightened. When you are facing your issues and growing and still you experience pain, the solution to save you is to remember that nothing works as well as carrying the light to someone who needs it. You are then saved again and again and are surrounded by forces of the universe that lift you into a higher context. The higher context sometimes makes your problems totally irrelevant, sometimes solves the problems or sometimes helps you live through the problems until you are able to sort them out. If anything else is the priority for the enlightened soul, then they are left with their own efforts to be the source of their own salvation.

Even when you may not feel the inspiration to carry the light to those who need it, when you do, it will save you. Returning to an experience of upset when there is no one to carry the light to is not a sign that something is wrong. Rather, it is merely the time to contend with your feelings.

You will be saved in a thousand countless ways each time you carry the light. Cumulatively this will remove you far from the condition of lost souls. You will recognize your deep love and devotion to the Source of this existence for having given you the very means to embrace your light at an ascendant level.

If you look at the Masters, past and current, you will find that they live in the same way. They have lost their interest in personal concerns and become entirely involved with their universal purpose. It is then that the gift of personal fulfillment is given to them for they are giving themselves to their universal purpose.

Some have tried to achieve this through ambition and it has not worked. Ambition only creates sickness of the kind we have mentioned. Some however, have truly found that their giving is their salvation and their meaning. Through their giving they have found freedom from the slavery of their own self-centeredness. When it is time for them to face issues having to do with their normal human life, they also face those with great grace.

– Astarte

SEPARATION

I see, feel and hear a lot that people want to be with me all the time, but I do not understand that. I do not understand the perception that there is a separation. If they are talking about something other than the truth that we are together now, I do not understand.

– God

SERENITY

I know how strong my will is and when I was here I learned I could do anything. There was nothing I could not do with my will except one thing, serenity. I could not get serenity with my will. I could have spiritual power, physical power, control, a certain amount of enlightenment, love, support and wonderful things, but when a soul believes they must control their universe to be happy, there is no serenity for them. That is like standing in the ocean and pushing the waves to the shore saying, "I am helping."

It is fine that the person is pushing the waves to the shore. Better they push the waves toward the shore than turn around and push them away saying, "I am stopping them," because that is even harder. But, what about the surfers who ride the waves and the people who understand what that ocean is for? They are much happier than those who are standing in that ocean pushing the waves to the shore saying, "I cannot get out or there will be no waves."

What I am saying is, life has its own direction. Find that direction because it is very, very easy. I know many say it is not, but it is easy. Just go through life using your wits and skills, but when you cannot, you just stand back immediately and say, "Let the Higher Will be made clear to me and give me the strength to go with it."

Now, you may still do the exact same thing or not, but when you are fighting, something is wrong and you may not know what it is. When you stand back and permit an expansive awareness to join you, you cannot go wrong.

– Sun Bear

SERVICE

To want to serve is to come a very long way. To long to serve is to come an even further way. To live to serve with love is to come even further still. And finally, to find the greatest pleasure in serving with love, is to have fulfilled the purpose of your path.

– Yeshua

❖❖❖

To embrace the totality of who you are as you grow in awareness takes more than loving and appreciating who you are now and who you are becoming, although those are very essential parts of it. To embrace the totality of who you are is also about serving, which is utilizing the awareness you come into in some way that contributes to life around you. Without that contribution you cannot get admitted as a peer with the eternal forces because the only way you can experience your being as eternal is if you give away what you come to know. Giving it away keeps the flow and the circuit going.

There is a certain dilemma that presents about becoming the master of your existence and a being who is also surrendered to a higher power. Creating your reality and surrendering to a higher power are two contradictory principles. How do you do both at once? How do you know which to do when? How do you know when it is time to take charge and focus and create the reality of your intention? How do you know when to stop doing that and allow something else to happen that may be beyond your own will?

Usually you do not know ahead of time which one to do. It is a matter of trying and seeing, putting forward your energy and if it works, you are supposed to master it. If it does not work, then you are supposed to let go. It is as simple as that and the wisdom is knowing which one to do when. It is a simple thing if you understand what is supporting you.

– Sun Bear

❖❖❖

There is one and only one primary purpose that needs to be embraced and it needs to be a constant. The purpose is the recognition that you are in existence for surrendering into your light through serving. Serving does not mean giving of the self from your own resource, but rather giving that which lifts you. That is, you give from the Infinite Resource into that dimension that needs it.

– Philos

❖❖❖

The definition of service is, that as a result of whatever experiences you have had that have brought awakening to you, you are motivated to do anything. Passing on the light creates life getting better and better. When you feel low and down and terrible, and believe me there is no such thing as being so high that you never face that, you will be in good enough spiritual condition to get through. But when you face those low places say, "Creator, show me the way to get my mind off my own problems yet again, and help me help somebody else."

Many will say that is avoiding yourself. Sometimes that is avoidance, but if you are my kind of spiritual aspirant you could use to get your mind off of yourself now and then. I never met anybody more self-centered then I when I was here. Most people in the final stages of their incarnations get very self-centered, my realization, my inspiration, my love, my focus, my aspiration, my desires, me, me, me, me, me, like an opera singer. That is very burdensome because you have mastered 'me'. Now it is time to get out of that, and when you do, everything flows.

– Merlin

❖❖❖

Through giving you see things about yourself that show you who you are. Serenity comes in this way because self-knowledge and self-acceptance are increased on those levels where some wounds now exist. It is also in this way that more support, love and light come.

– Chief Great White Eagle, Sun Bear, with Miriam

❖❖❖

In order for you to progress further it is very important that your focus is on how you can give away what you have received. That is why you have it because the more you give it away the more you will get.

What you are not in control of is who receives it and who wants it. What you are in control of is how you can give away the beauty that is inside of you from which so many can get so much. That is what the Creator gave to you and this is the source of your serenity.

– *Chief Great White Eagle, Sun Bear, with Miriam*

❖❖❖

For those who are about their purpose, all that is egocentric in them shall be surrendered, for it must be. This means the development of an utterly loving devotion to service, which is helping a soul who reaches out to take their step into the light with no thought of the self. This act is what it means to become one with service.

As this unfolds, it is inevitable that an awakened and enlightened soul, if honest, becomes acutely aware of all of their wounds. So many and so deep are these wounds as to make them think that the obstacles that must be transcended are insurmountable. What seems to be insurmountable appears relentlessly again and again and again until such time and in whatever way they are able to find that part of their being that lovingly exists for one intent: to embrace and help another suffering soul into their light. It is for one reason that this comes about and that is because they realize that they too have been helped in this way.

– *Yeshua*

❖❖❖

Speaking from my own experience as a Shaman, the reason to serve and surrender is so that you can have a good life. You will see serenity in places in your life that will shock you and find yourself at peace with things that used to drive you crazy. You will also notice that you move through difficulties very quickly because you are in your own flow of Spirit. It will not give you what you want, but It will give you what you need.

Many people clench here because that is where their fear of the universe comes up. But there are things that you need, which are such precious gifts, that you do not even know you need. It will feel so good to feel these things coming toward you and to feel that wonderful love coming out of you. Simultaneously, losses will occur and sometimes you will grieve, but your hands will be so full of what you needed that inside you will be glad. You will understand that the Great Spirit is taking away from you what you could not let go of yourself.

Walking with the Spirit becomes a constant conscious experience, but you cannot control it. The only thing that keeps you in it is the desire to serve, to keep letting go, to keep finding that place in your heart that loves to commune with the love of the Great Spirit and then to give it away.

You can only give love to those who want it, not to those whose time is not yet. Your heart may want to give it to someone who is not yet ready to receive it from you, but you cannot. You cannot deliver a person into the light, but you can carry the light to the person if they are ready or able to receive it. You will feel glad and humble that you have been able to bring such a life saving light to your brothers and sisters of this world. I cannot begin to convey to you any description of the power and the beauty that occur from this act.

– Sun Bear

❖❖❖

The time shall come when not only utter surrender becomes the practice, but service also becomes the ultimate dedication of your existence. Service is knowing that your primary purpose is to help another cross over from darkness into light, from aloneness into wholeness, from woundedness into healing and into the hands of the Creator.

Where that is your primary purpose, you shall see how all other things shall come to you. If you ask to let go of whatever stands in the way of that service, all of the heavens themselves will help you let go. Your relationships and all of your world affairs will be brought into balance one way or another.

You shall not be made to suffer if you can remember that you are here, not only for the purpose of service, but also to gain oneness and joy in your union with the Creator. Because that joy and union become important to you, you will be willing to face whatever lessons need to be faced.

– Chief Great White Eagle, Sun Bear, with Miriam

SHADOW

At some point near the pinnacle of your completion of stepping through the doorway into your ascendant nature, the light embraces you so totally that there is no shadow self to be found for a time. This is a powerful awakening that is given so that you can remember what that experience is like. Then you let go of that experience and rest in your humanity, walking in God consciousness, hand in hand with the light and the shadow. Thus, your shadow self cannot be eliminated, but rather only illuminated.

These peak experiences of God consciousness occur as a result of what you go through. The experiences put to rest your resentment and anger, which are fears that there will not be what you need in the universe and the hurts such as, "God, how could you have allowed me to feel such pain?" That is why an experience of God consciousness comes because it reveals an inexplicable experience that puts that anger and resentment to rest. You are then returned to normal human experience after having been re-created.

– Jhenrhett Turonok

❖❖❖

The first thing I wish to say is life works. There is not an opportunity for fatal error. But, there is the dark side that walks with the light, a shadow self that walks everywhere a human being goes. The dark side exists to keep you humble enough to see the Great Spirit. When you get too far in your ego, you cannot see the Great Spirit anymore. To see the Great Spirit, there has to be softness and receptivity in your heart. The shadow self keeps you honest, questioning yourself and your nature.

The time comes when the shadow self is befriended, when the weapons are laid down and it holds no more strength. The time comes when the shadow self is almost a friend.

The shadow self cannot be fought. If you try to resist the shadow self or fight with it, it always gets bigger. If the shadow self is heard and asked, "What do you want?" sometimes it just shrivels down and says, "Nothing." Then you come into right order and are able to see the presence of the Great Spirit. But, when the shadow self is fought or mistaken for the truth of who you are, blowing up out of proportion, the Great Spirit disappears. You can then have a very painful existence.

– Sun Bear, Chief, Tall Trees, Two Trees, Sky Walker, Sam Strong Body, Red Sky and many others

❖❖❖

Walking hand and hand with your own demons in a radiant light is a spiritual awakening. As you recognize within yourself your own shadow side and learn to live with it rather than trying to purge yourself of it, you gain true spiritual power. When you no longer fear these deadly forces that lie within, there will be no more terror, which oftentimes happens in stages.

– Sun Bear, Chief Great White Eagle

❖❖❖

In my life as Sun Bear, sometimes I had to look at the dark side because it was where I was growing. At first I would think something was wrong. I would then realize, "Oh yes, I have to do my work now. That darkness is the existing place where faith has not gotten yet."

– Sun Bear

SHARING

There are two ways in which people reach others: by offering what appear to be answers and by offering a way to accept, which comes through the sharing of experiences, strength and hope.

The more powerful way to reach others is offering the strength and hope that come from your experiences. This way is more truth and it addresses the angst and the emptiness. It gives hope and allows a soul to be open to their own direct communion with the Infinite where their personal misery is resolved on a day-by-day basis. Life then becomes an experience of learning and receiving rather than a painful resentment and demanding. That is a tremendous gift to offer, a treasure that can only be offered to sick, suffering souls by those who have experienced it. Offering this gift is the greater thing and it is this that clears away karma, bringing fulfillment that is beyond the imagination of any soul.

– Miriam, QuanYin and Astarte

SIMPLICITY

It can be torturous to you if there is anything other than the seeking of a simple and humble life. This must be the priority, then all other things shall come. Through simplicity you will be able to serve and let go of whatever must be let go of when the time comes to let it go. If there is a great and sophisticated mental paradigm with many requirements and needs, then letting go can be torturous. If the orientation is humble and simple, then it is not difficult to let go and the way through is more easily seen and embraced. It is easy then to let go of the resistance and embrace acceptance and all of the support that will be provided by the world around you as a result of your surrender.

– Yeshua

SOUL MATE

I am very glad that I never knew about this soul mate business when I was here. Two souls come together for business and they exchange, complete and move on.

Human beings have projected onto the soul mate principle this whole notion of romance in which sexual and emotional needs get fulfilled. Sexual and emotional fulfillment are genuine needs that the Great Spirit put there to help human beings survive. A soul mate however, could be any kind of relationship: friend, teacher, daughter, father, etc. Soul mate is a soul union where ideas of romance usually will not work. It is most rare to get a soul mate relationship where ideas of romance can work.

Relationships of a romantic kind may or may not be of a soul mate kind, but they are necessary. The relationships start out mostly in the same way and sooner or later, whether it is a soul mate or not, it can become an annoyance. Then, if you want the relationship rather than need it, you must find unconditional love and forgiveness, even when the other person will not change for you and you do not like the way they are. You must love them even when they will not be what your needs project onto them.

The only difference between a soul mate and non soul mate relationship at the highest level is that with a soul mate there is a powerful and compelling soul's purpose. There continue to be spiritual breakthroughs of growth, regardless of how romantic the relationship, if it is a soul mate. If a relationship is not a soul mate relationship, and your needs are not getting met, then it is empty and useless.

A soul mate relationship does not emotionally fulfill you just because it is a soul mate. Being in relationship to each other is meaningful because there is karmic business and therefore a reason to exist beyond the nominal physical instincts and it has a richness to it.

– Sun Bear

❖❖❖

This is the truth about love: it hurts to give away someone that you love because you do not know if you will ever get them back. When you let go of someone you love, if it is an important love to have, that love will come back and live with you forever. In our people we call that our relations. Relations cannot go away because you have soul strings connecting you and you can never come apart.

That is what soul mates are, gifts from the Creator to each other for all eternity. There is no more separation of time and space. That is why it is said, "What God has brought together no one can rend asunder." It cannot be done.

The realization of that is a learned awakening. It must be learned over and over again until the absoluteness of that transcends every other kind of experience. The truth of the eternal realm can only be realized because of love of that kind. It is so between whoever is your soul mate and it is also exactly the same between you and the Great Spirit.

That realization, having been understood, is the same dynamic and energy as it is to be one with God eternally. It is an absolute reality of the truth, and no other truth exists except that. Even though that truth may have been aided by being expressed through a person or persons, when it is understood it does not make any difference any more if it is a person or Great Spirit. The love becomes exactly the same thing and you cannot make it without that realization.

You are held together with your soul mate until you both make it. Soul cords keep returning you back together regardless of the dimensions or worlds you are each in and regardless of who is incarnated or not. You must come together until all parts are absolute in the Great Spirit. In fact that is why your Spirit Guides come to you regardless of that you are supposedly in the physical and we are supposedly in the spiritual. The veil or warp between dimensions disappears and makes the seeming separation between the physical reality of your dimension and the spiritual reality of ours immaterial. That reality must grow stronger and stronger until there is total certainty for you.

– Sun Bear and Chief Great White Eagle

❖❖❖

Old souls always have extraordinary and unusual relationships. Old souls do not necessarily get married and live happily ever after just like that. They have a God experience that is far outside of the understanding of the day and true soul mates have those experiences too. Soul mate relationships bring up your relationship with God for examination and healing. These relationships force you into the God experience.

Old souls can have simple relationships, although they usually have complex ones. If they want a simple relationship, they must find a simple person who knows how to love and they must swallow their own complexity. The simple one who knows how to love better just keeps coming back and saying, "But I love you, I just love you."

Yeshua had to have a simple, simple woman, but one who was wise beyond all measure. Yeshua was not a simple man although he thought he was until he found out what real simplicity was. Her love was profound, leaving him speechless, and he was rarely speechless.

– Sun Bear, Chief, Tall Trees, Two Trees, Sky Walker, Sam Strong Body, Red Sky and many others

❖❖❖

Soul mate style relationship is one of unconditional love in which both people are in the practice of letting go. Both people know that there is no way to own the relationship even though they will feel promised to each other. They will also carry in the nature of this experience that which will clearly reflect that they are unable to put many limitations on it. They will both need to be free to be who they are and willingly give all to each other.

– Jhenrhett Turonok

❖❖❖

Soul mate relationships are not perfect relationships, but they have a decidedly different quality. A soul mate relationship occurs when two individuals feel whole and feel as though all they wish to do is give. They have touched within themselves that which they are and what it is they are about. They are in the mode of giving that and knowing that this is why they are alive. They are in so much appreciation of who they are that they enjoy their being one day at a time in a rich and powerful experience of love, and they love expressing that for which they are here. When the persons in this relationship to themselves and to life also meet each other, they are in the mode of giving and feel tremendously given to in the presence of the other so that there is never the need in a sense, to ask to be given to.

– Philos

SOUL'S BUSINESS

The business for which you are here, which is a soul's business, is to complete things that you have not yet completed. You are not here to have a life based on what you see that others have or based on what you might imagine are the answers to your instinctual drives. If you become involved with, as a primary purpose, controlling your existence so that you can enjoy it, you could find yourself going to your grave never having enough control to enjoy it. To fully enjoy your existence, the solution is far beyond the manipulation of the physical events in life to attempt to meet your needs.

– Astarte and Miriam

SPIRIT GUIDES

Everyone has Guides who are communicating with them, whether they realize it or not. We just communicate in different ways than with a mouth and vocal cords. When you become sensitive enough by noticing the little signs that kind of push you, then you begin to recognize what seems to be our voice.

We do not come to arrange your life for you. In fact, we do not even come around until you begin to think about things broader than your own life, things of planetary and universal order beyond, "Who shall I marry," and "What job do I get next?" That is when we come, but we will come around sometimes for those other things if we see that those things are standing in the way of the more important purpose for which you are here. But, if you only ask us to help work out some of the mundane things of life, then we disappear back to where we live.

You get our attention when you begin to focus on things that have to do with either raising the consciousness of this plane in some way, its individuals or things that have to do with healing the pain that many are in. That is when you begin to feel, "I am getting some guidance here." Anyone interested in communicating consciousness from other dimensions like art, music or channeling also gets our attention. You will always find artists who know they are not the ones who are doing the painting. Many musicians say, "I did not write that. It wrote itself."

As soon as someone says, "I think something helps me," then we come in very strongly because all we need is just a little acknowledgment. Our purpose is not to prove our existence to you, but to get you linked up with what we are linked up with, which is Great Spirit.

Your Guides want to talk to you, so listen for them. Some people have been trying to listen, but feel that they have not heard from their Guides. To hear, you have to be very versatile with consciousness itself. In other words, we would not come and move a table unless we did it with someone's body. If it becomes necessary, all right we will do it, but that is a great expenditure of energy. It is much simpler for us to communicate with you if you get in touch with your own consciousness. Within your consciousness is where we speak. We speak in the higher frequencies of your own awareness. You must become well versed in those subtleties.

Get used to feeling the whispers of consciousness that come in your meditation because that also helps you hear from us. We give you messages through your dreams, for that is the easiest mediation between your world and ours. Sometimes you can use empowered statements such as, "I am one with God now." You have to say things like that to get our attention because positive intention and affirmation makes you noticeable to Spirit. These positive things bring you out of the very negatively aimed mass consciousness that unfortunately many people think is truth.

The common agreement, which is usually very negative, says that things do not look too good in the world. That is just a consensus, not the truth. It is just a point of view that many people agree with because people are very fearful for their own survival. That fear is a strong charge that makes all fear amplified in their minds and wherever they see it, it seems like truth. Those who affirm positive realities begin to come away from the fear and begin to see things in a very different way, not too positively or too negatively.

Voices or impressions come from your higher Spirit Guides, but believe me, there is some lower guidance too. The voices or the impressions from higher spiritual guidance always say things through your awareness and into your being that are intelligent, wise, loving and empowering. If you hear a voice saying, "Stupid, stupid, person, you never should have done that," that is not a Guide. That voice is just an energy of consciousness you might give into that will not lead you in the higher path.

To get in touch with Guides listen for the wisest, kindest, most empowering voices in your own mind. Start paying attention to those voices and then before you know it, a little psychic door will open in your being and you will be able to hear and see us. You have to have the eyes to see, which means you have to get into our frequency.

There is no reason why you should get in touch with us. We are available to you if you clear out the rusty channel. So, if you are prepared to do that work, your connection will be strong and true.

– Chief Great White Eagle

❖❖❖

Our dimension intertwines with your own. We are not far away. You visit us all the time and your awareness reaches out and calls to us. We respond to you and you respond to us. Every now and then, when you look around, you think you see something. Every now and then you will know that you are aware and that you feel our presence there with you in a kind of comfort place. We know that you do not always experience us as concrete, but we know that you sense our presence around you and it is your consciousness that is touched.

Remember that consciousness is not only here in what you think is your mind. Your mind is everywhere, not just here, and consciousness is in every single part of your body. Your consciousness and your body are in an entire room and beyond because consciousness is everywhere.

– Merlin

❖❖❖

The purpose of contacting your Spiritual Guides is so that we can guide you, shining the way to your spiritual awareness. Thus, our primary purpose with you oftentimes is to get you to ask the right questions. I do not mean necessarily that you go around asking questions, but that you are inwardly alert to what is the right direction.

For example, there is a question that people sometimes ask themselves in order to get some clarity. “Why is it that I find myself in destructive relationships time and time again?” That seems like a very good question, but if that person has asked that question time and time again and still does not know why, they are asking the wrong question.

The question is rarely a 'why' question. Better questions are, "How can I create constructive relationships? How can I have the relationship I want? How can I let go of destructive relationships?" Not, "Why am I in one?" What can be the answer to that question besides, "You fool, you stupid idiot," over and over again? All that can do is lead you to finding out something about yourself that you do not love when you ask those questions. It is better to ask, “How can I go in the direction that is right for me?”

The 'why' questions come out of a fundamental predetermination that something is wrong with you. It is like saying, “Really, what is the real secret here. I know there is something wrong with me, so tell me why I end up in these bad situations?” When somebody says the right thing (of course the right thing being that you have known there is something wrong with you, like you are not smart enough, good enough, pretty enough, tall enough or thin enough) it agrees with your presumed negative outcome. These are terrible questions to be asking. The right questions to ask are questions that presume there is an enlightened response. You must presume that there is a light and that predetermination aims you in the right direction.

Our purpose is to get you oriented so that you can learn to be alert for the higher opportunities and to point you in directions where there is light on your path. But, we can do nothing if the questions you ask are lousy. Your questions must be answered according to the way you ask them because if we give another reply you will not even notice it. The only thing you will be attentive to is the kind of question that you ask. You will discount any other inner or outer response because you are not pointed in the right way.

To get you to be alerted to the right things we drop all kinds of clues. We answer questions particularly so that the remaining unknown gets you asking another question, perhaps a better one. If we can get you to ask the right questions, you will get the right answers.

The way you want to approach going inward to receive your Guides is to orient your consciousness toward the most important life concern going on for you with an attitude that there is a light at the end of the tunnel. We are glad to give you insights into things of lesser importance because sometimes those are important, even though they may be important in a lesser way. But, you can only receive the highest guidance if you ask the highest questions.

Sometimes you force one of two things to happen if you do not ask the highest questions. One thing is that you ask a lower form of consciousness, who does care about those kinds of things, to respond to you. Two is that you force us to give up the most expanded way we work to become something smaller just to reach you.

All it is that we come here to do is to reach into the core of your being to get you to be alert to the presence of your spirit self and your connectedness and oneness to God. We want to come to you in a meaningful way that will help you understand what your life is about and to help you take the next steps. We want this to be revealed to you and do not want to tell you what to do. We want you to understand what is right for you so that you do not have to go around in unknowing.

Now, oftentimes in contacting your Spiritual Guides you may not actually get the Guide, but you might get signs, symbols, sounds, sensations, feelings, visions, pieces of phrases, names and things of this kind. You might snatch from the consciousness whatever you can. It is very quick. You may be thinking and thinking and not know anything, then something comes and you return to thinking and thinking and forget the in-between part.

What you must do is learn to snatch the little particles that come to you from that zone. That is why it is important sometimes to meditate because it is like a snatching frenzy. Let us say you go into the space and you have all kinds of thoughts, but then you start picking up little pieces, phrases, images, feelings, sensations, understandings and energies. When you ask a question you go in with a specific focus and you get a specific answer. Both of these things are necessary.

You cannot always go in asking questions for the reason that you may not have the awareness to ask the sufficiently highest questions. If all you go inside for is to ask questions, you may be asking questions that do not really serve you. Meditations get you to evolve in that space and to raise your consciousness so that other times when you ask questions they get higher and higher. You then ask better and better questions, thus both kinds of inner contacts are necessary.

– Philos

❖❖❖

We who are Guides for you are fiercely determined to touch into your consciousness and draw you beyond the ideas that you have defined as yourself. We cause you to confront your beliefs about self, love and life. We are here to lead you to challenges that cause you to recognize within your own consciousness the truth of this existence. We do not wish to bring struggle or strife to you, which is never our intention. Challenges are meant to be exciting and stimulating. We wish to raise your awareness to be alert, to provoke you to ask questions about yourself and life.

You are not here to seek answers. You are here to ask questions. You will find many solutions and come to many understandings, but you are not here to accumulate theories of existence and to understand all of the metaphysical principles of life. You are here to grasp those aspects of life that are meaningful to you.

You are not here to study until you know all of the answers, but rather to learn how to be comfortable and be at peace with questions that are unanswered. Only if you are at peace with a paradox can you know truth. If you have no room in your being to have questions that have no answers, then you will put answers where none belong. As such, you will make up your truth and design your own karma from which you must break away and transcend. If you are the kind of entity who realizes that ascension, consciousness and awakening mean that your awareness is curious, inquisitive, and alert, then you will gain understanding.

– Philos

SPIRITUAL EXPERIENCES

Spiritual experiences are any experiences that foster a sense of trust and faith in your being.

– Chief Great White Eagle and Sun Bear

SPIRITUALITY

Beware of someone telling you that your spirituality will fix everything in your life so that nothing goes wrong. You can be the most spiritually awakened person on the planet and things can still go terribly wrong. A spiritual person will be able to let go of that without comparing it to who they are.

– Chief Great White Eagle, Sun Bear, and Miriam

❖❖❖

When you are getting confused, you need enough honesty to say, "I am confused," or, "That is not what I am about. I am about God, Spirit, love and giving. That is who I am." That is spirituality and that is the straight talk with God.

– Chief Great White Eagle, Sun Bear, and Miriam

SPIRITUAL ASCENSION

Spiritual ascension requires much more than a focus upon an inner Divine Source of power and light. Ascension requires a surrender to that Supreme Intelligence and letting go completely to the guidance of that inner light. This inner light is free of all personal ambition, drive and directive that stands in the way and leads to many, many troubles. Rare is the soul who wants to give up their own personality to discover what is revealed by the Source, which may have something else to show and may create a total psychic change.

This shifting simply means that in order to complete your human life, you must be prepared to complete the karmas, not only of this life, but of all of your existences. It means the revelation of a kind of love that is truly altruistic. Your love must eventually become a love that is without conditions or limits because it is impossible to achieve completion without such a nature of love. Only when you are possessed of enough love to give to others before yourself, even in others' eyes to sacrifice for someone else because you are so filled with love, are you able to have enough power to pay the karmic debts, thereby allowing yourself to complete your human life in this or any other incarnation.

You must be prepared to go to any lengths to fill yourself with such love so that you are able to give unselfishly when needed without having a thought or a feeling of the very natural state of self-centeredness that every human being experiences. The natural human self, while still in a human body, becomes surrendered to an unnatural human state of ascendant awareness. When a sufficient number of beings in this world simultaneously make that shift or over time, each one makes that shift a possibility for many, many more to enter that doorway.

This is not a state that can be aspired to, for to hold an aspiration toward that will stand in the way. However, what you can aspire to that is a part of the ascendant reality that brings the necessary power and grace, is to devotionally approach the Supreme through the inner doorway in your being. You then ask of the Supreme to remove your own self-centeredness and to be made an instrument of the Divine to bring peace and light into this world with no thought of yourself, but for that which includes all. In that sense, the love is truly an altruistic love.

In no way does this kind of consciousness match or parallel in any way what is naturally motivating to human beings. It is only motivating to those who have touched such supreme awareness that it creates within them a desire for that kind of love. They have found, through their lifetimes of incarnations, that every other kind of love has failed. They are driven to the ascendant self with an aspiration given to them for that supreme love as a result of their divine experience.

With these two driving inspirations, the love and the pain of the world, they are then moved to an ascendant reality that for them is real, but for others it does not exist. The Creator brings to that soul all of their needs in that state of being. A soul that is not truly ready, or is not yet ascendant burns up in that kind of life and cannot achieve it. This life is then best forgotten as an aspiration and you will instead be brought to the Supreme Light by your desire to love and serve. That consciousness grows within you until you are ready and able for more. Readiness is brought to you, if you seek it, through asking the Spirit to make this revelation known to you. Subsequently your experiences will lead you to sufficient spiritual experiences to make you able to survive such an altruistic love in a world that does not support it.

– Yeshua

SPIRITUAL JOURNEY

The ascendant path is a mighty, mighty journey, which is the biggest step of human evolution that remains. There will be a few changes in the human physical body, but not that many. The remaining changes will result because of the shifts people are making emotionally, spiritually and mentally. Some people have already experienced what that does to their DNA and their body. The DNA and genetic structure are nothing but encoded thinking. DNA is the chemical product of a collective or individual psychology that is passed on from generation to generation. When an individual breaks that code, that code is then changed for all.

Most human beings cannot get far enough to get the DNA code to shift. The changes never filter down to the genetic structure and only changes the most superficial kinds of physiological responses, except every now and then when you hear of an extraordinary case of spontaneous remission of diseases and healing. Because that is an exception rather than the rule, many people think that the rule is the biological law, but biological law is only a terrestrial agreement. There are some aspects of this law that are the common agreement of human beings, and some aspects of this law are the common agreement of all life forms on the planet. In either case, it is a common agreement. Everyone is tied into a frequency of energy through their thoughts and it seems you must abide by certain laws of the physical universe.

Occasionally there are people who come into your world whose path is to challenge those laws or to discover something unknown about those laws. Until that time those precepts, theories and ideas seemed to be lost until somebody had enough persistence, intelligence or awareness to see that there was another law underlying the existing law that either supported or invalidated the existing law. Sometimes these people are all by themselves and nobody believes them so they seem to be crazy. Maybe they have to be a little bit crazy to see things differently. Maybe you have to get a little outside of yourself (the self you believe is yourself, the one that is running the show most of the time) in order to see things differently. Getting outside of yourself is a part of what the spiritual journey absolutely requires. In this way one or two new laws or perceptions can pop in amidst the tens of thousands of pre-existing laws.

The spiritual journey is where you begin to explore these things that you would not have looked at because they seemed to be too far outside of existing standards. Some breakthroughs in all areas are found by building on top of existing understanding, but when it comes to spirituality this world has a long way to go. There is a whole lot of room to get outside of existing understanding to find out what is so.

– *Sun Bear*

SPIRITUAL VIRTUE

The greatest spiritual virtue is courage to face what is ahead and to be shown something that is greater. This is simple but not easy and it exercises to the maximum your faith and trust that the light will not fail you now, even though you are sorely tested. Your willingness to be shown something that does not now exist will save you. You cannot find that something within your current identity because it does not exist there, which is why you will feel that you cannot find it. Hence, the ascendant nature comes in to be revealed.

– Jhenrhett Turonok

STRUGGLE

Ceasing to struggle is indeed a challenge in a time of great personal and global transition. It is an art. Be gentle with yourself as you embrace freedom from struggle. This art begins as a craft. Crafts are a work-a-day kind of thing and an art is a craft taken to the highest level where it becomes gracious. You can raise the craft of living to an art form.

– Philos

SUFFERING

An entity who stands apart entirely from the current consensus, who is in no way like the other human beings in this world, would be so utterly rejected by this world as to be of no use to the world. Therefore, all human beings existing in this world must carry a certain level of wounding until there is enough healing to create a shift in the consensus archetypal thinking.

Because you carry that wounding it will undoubtedly appear in some way again and again and cannot be gotten rid of entirely so long as you are in this world. The object therefore is not to rid yourself of the wounding, but rather to recognize the wounding and surrender it to the Supreme. So long as you are a human being, you will find yourself surrendering the wounding again and again, which shatters your ego, which seeks to be perfect.

When you no longer seek the perfection that your ego drives you to seek, then amazing and saving grace will rescue you time and time again. That is why there is such a song called Amazing Grace because a soul feels wretched again and again even though it is not. But, once you witness such experiences of salvation again and again, you are free and no longer vulnerable to suffering. When pain comes, either you have the strength to be able to meet it or you miraculously experience grace lifting you from the condition that seems flawed and inevitable.

Most of the people who are angry with the Creator are angry because the world seems hopelessly flawed. They wonder how it can be that a loving Creator would allow suffering. They still have a defiant ego and have not yet the humility to embrace the power of the Creator that lifts them from that condition. Grace is unable to reach them so long as they carry that level of identification with the false self. Whoever experiences suffering, is in this place.

– Yeshua

SUPPORT

The Creator wants you to be able to say, "The whole thing that supports me is the light and love of God. There is not a single person, penny, substance or anything in my life that has not been given to me by the Source." The Creator wants you to have that experience because you want that experience and because in that experience you will have your oneness forever. The hard part is that in order to get that way, some of what needs to happen will not always feel so good along the way. Those interim times are where the Creator wants us to support you.

The basic principle is this: the Creator wants you totally supported, knowing that everything that supports you comes from an infinite, irresistible force with which nothing can interfere. Then all you need to do is be confident by asking for the will of the Creator, taking that above all other influence.

The will of the Creator may be different tomorrow than the will of the Creator today, so it just needs to be for today. Say, "Creator, guide me in what is Your will today." At the end of that day thank the Creator and then it is finished.

The next day will hold a different adventure and you ask for the will for that day and go with that. In this way, the aspect of the ego that gets in the way of intuitively knowing what the will of the Creator is deteriorates day by day. Before you know it you are always in the will of the Creator because there is receptivity along with a constant prayer, a constant asking and a constant expression of it.

– Sun Bear

❖❖❖

Changes in the psyche that deeply and profoundly affect your emotions and psychic stabilities are attended by Spirit, by those who are termed Spiritual Guides. But we are just Guides and not those who can move you from darkness to light. We can only point out the way and say, "Go here, go there." We cannot force you to do what we think is right and we cannot keep you from what we think is wrong. We can only attend to you whereby whatsoever you choose, be it right or wrong, if you have sought the will and help of the Creator, then we can bring about a higher result from any choice you have made. This is what we do.

The help that is brought to you manifests itself from all quarters. It comes in the form of help and support from friends or strangers, offered sometimes in the most peculiar ways. Sometimes the help may not seem to directly address any issue of particular concern to you, but rather simply the presence of assistance shall be there. The assistance shall come in the form of opportunities and the form of gifts that shall manifest. It shall also come in the form of light that affects others who enter into your presence. Others will be drawn to you for all manner of reasons that may or may not be of relevance to you. These gifts of Spirit shall manifest for those who seek surrender.

– Yeshua

SUPREME CONSCIOUSNESS

Supreme consciousness is not knowing everything all the time. Supreme consciousness is embracing what you would rather embrace and letting go of that which you would rather let go. At least for human beings it is like that. You have a gift of choice in order to claim, identify and embrace what you want, and a gift to choose to let go of what you want. Both gifts are gifts of your awareness and memory.

– Merlin

SURRENDER

The slow relinquishing of the focus upon the self is the most fearful surrender of all of humankind and is the final lifting. It can usually only occur in stages, for it is often revealed in stages, and the willingness only comes in stages.

– Miriam, QuanYin, and Astarte

❖❖❖

You are never completely surrendered now and forever. Surrender is a moment-to-moment experience. So long as you know such a thing as time, yesterday's total surrender could be ended by tomorrow's complete shutting down. The only thing that allows you to be surrendered totally is the level of your true and spiritual awakening.

Awakening is the result of having accumulated many experiences that bring realization and actualization. Realization means understanding and actualization means understanding in practice such that life reflects your realizations. This reflection comes from accumulated spiritual and world experiences that bring such a level of awakening that you can never go back from that awakening.

– Philos

❖❖❖

It takes great courage and many prayers to surrender to that which is greater than yourself. But you must surrender because your will alone is not nearly enough to embrace the truth of what you are. You must petition to intertwine your will with that which is expansive beyond your knowing, beyond that which you even know that you know. There is what you know that you know, and what you know that you do not know. There is also what you do not know that you do not know. You must petition what you do not know that you do not know to intertwine Itself into your reality or you will be unable to pull yourself from the rest of what is around you.

– Dormor

⁂

I do not know what the Great Spirit might consider to be in the way of your complete surrender. All I know is that every one of us who has ascended has said that we just did not expect it to be the particular thing it was. No matter how we were all told by our teachers, we just never expected what occurred. Great Spirit has a way of finding these things. I am saying this because I know Great Spirit can sneak up from behind. God is very good at doing that. However I also know that Great Spirit has a way of giving you far more than you ever even knew to ask for. That is what gets built and only your faith allows you to keep going.

– Sun Bear

⁂

So particular are the rules of Spirit in this dimension that the whole picture cannot be known at this time by any. The clever movements of God through this dimension are to relax the grip that the consciousness of human beings has upon the darkness so that they might instead embrace the light.

It is only possible for people to serve the light when they continuously surrender. Surrender occurs through prayer and meditation and sometimes through chanting, fasting and other spiritual devotion. Such acts fortify and awaken spiritual experiences so that there is a lasting awakening.

– Chief Great White Eagle, Sun Bear, with Miriam

⁂

The nature of surrender is only completely understood in that time when you have surrendered. In that time the surrendered is for now. When the surrender turns out to be forever, it shall turn out to be that way.

– Yeshua

⁂

On those days when you are in surrender, enjoy it and even announce it to the world if you wish. Say, "Come with me, I know God. This day there is much of me to share. Here, those of you who are able to receive, I give this freely. Take this, for I keep my spiritual condition by giving it away."

On these days you will know God and the voice of God's Spirit shall be strong in you and teach you things and embrace you. The very next day it may not be there and you may be but an ordinary being, but where there is surrender you will say, "Thank you for this ordinary day." There will be great appreciation and great fulfillment and no less joy for you on these days.

You will see many kinds of days. You will see many dimensions of your nature: greatness, smallness, perfection, flawed self. You will accept all of these days, which will be your humility. Your daily prayer will be, "My Creator, take all of me, the good or the bad. Take all aspects of me that stand in the way of my usefulness to you and my fellow humans. Grant me the strength, as I go forward from here, to do your bidding." You will see that this great unnamable resource is your friend, for it is permissive. All things are allowed.

– *Yeshua*

❖❖❖

It is important to make a decision to surrender your being to the Cosmic Truth as you have come to understand it, no matter how limited your understanding. As a result of making this decision, which is not the same as the act of surrender, but is simply a decision, the necessary acts come. The necessary acts come from accepting that each and every day, as a result of your decision to surrender, you are then seeking directly from the Supreme within yourself how you should act for that day in order to surrender. The Spirit speaks to you as to how to go forward and then helps you go forward.

You then have to stop fighting and struggling with the world and everyone in it, for that only creates more to account for later, more to set right, more to complete. If you cannot stop fighting, then say to the Spirit, "Show me the way. I would rather be about the business of completing."

After this is done, you can then see that everything that happens to you each day is an opportunity to settle affairs. One by one by one each and every affair is ultimately settled with the most unconditional love that you can find, which is a different amount for each soul.

The guidance within you shows you how to settle affairs and then gives you the power to do so, sometimes just barely. Matter by matter, you complete and create no new charge or karma. By grace, the angels and the powers of Spirit, you are helped to settle the many matters that you are unable to settle for yourself. You then do not have to return to this world time after time to complete unfinished business or karmas.

– *Yeshua*

❖❖❖

If your choice is to continue to be surrendered just for today that is the only thing to do. "Today I will surrender again to the lessons of the Great Spirit. I am willing to let go of the parts of me that keep me from surrendering to the Great Spirit for today." Today's surrender is not what you let go of yesterday or what you might have to let go of permanently tomorrow, but just the things for today. "For today I will surrender again." Today is the only place there is.

– *Chief Great White Eagle*

❖❖❖

In the morning ask for guidance that you be surrendered to the highest intent. Ask that all that stands at that highest intent include care and nurture of yourself and others. Ask that you freely give up all that stands in the way of that, asking for assistance in letting it go.
At the end of each day, give thanks for having been guided through that day. Whatever other prayer comes, pray this one and this shall help greatly.

– *Philos*

❖❖❖

When you reach to the God Light, you focus with your intention on the light and develop power and skill at doing so. Those who have a proclivity for the light, even though they may not consciously focus their intention and will, may also be absorbed by the light. Proclivities for the light may not come from their will, but from other experiences and learning situations in this and other lives.

When you do reach with this power and skill into that which is so much greater than you, you must simply surrender all conscious concerns into the vast scheme of things, ultimately completely becoming a part of that order. Indeed, that which may have brought you to that point of such great power and skill may then become an obstacle, interfering with the flow and creating chaos and disruptions. It is hard for the individual who is at that point of evolution to truly understand that their surrender is in fact a part of the higher order that seems to create chaotic forces.

You must let go of trying to figure out what is going on. Instead, you must develop clearer and clearer communions with the Divine, developing such faith and trust that the knowing within your awareness becomes the most powerful experience above and beyond all other.

The unknowing may never entirely go away and it is not supposed to, which is not to say however, that unknowing equals doubt. Doubt stems from fear or insecurity about your direction and purpose. These doubts and fears are signals there is yet more to uncover, more to learn, and more to surrender into. It is for this reason humility is necessary and must be cultivated. Without humility you cannot acknowledge insecurities, fears and doubts. With humility such things are recognized as opportunities to learn more and are signs that a great teaching is now at hand.

– *Philos*

SURVIVAL

There are many ways that you must learn to survive without knowing how to survive from the highest place. Some of these ways of surviving work like a bridge to get from one point to the next, but from time to time you will find that some of these ways no longer work. It is then that a different road is necessary, based upon the enlightenment that you have come to by way of experience. The past must then be forgiven, not judged.

– *Philos*

SWEAT FOR COMPENSATION

Everything you have done in terms of relationship, money and work, you have earned and it has been sweat for compensation. That is not how it is supposed to be. You have not yet experienced being given to freely in terms of money, love or anything else, which is the shift to the fourth dimension.

– *Chief Great White Eagle*

TALKING TO GREAT SPIRIT

When you are speaking, depending on what you are asking, Great Spirit is receiving you. The Source hears one kind of message because only one kind of message is powerful enough and big enough to reach It in the truth. Everything else, other than that kind of thing, is not even real to the Creator. It is the product of some other hallucination that Creator cannot acknowledge, which comes from living in this dimension. The Source hears when you say the kind of thing that is very broad. The thing that Creator acknowledges and receives directly is along the lines of, "Your will be done, not mine," and "Help me to let go to that, Creator."

Other things that are also for your good are received by the agent that is able to help. This is where you actually reach us, even though you are directing it toward the Creator, which helps you be received by higher forces. "Creator, I really need a new car," may never get to the Source, but because you directed it there the higher agents will help it come about. The Creator will not know or will not really care to know about the car, even though on one level It will because what is known to us is known by the Creator. To the Creator, many things do not matter because the Creator is in a state of being where nothing matters. To us, something matters because that is the reason we exist. We exist for the purpose of serving.

The hardest thing is to keep remembering that what you truly want is the will of the Great Spirit. You can only remember this if your version of the Great Spirit is one who loves you. Many people hold an image of the Great Spirit that they fear and then they cannot truly pray to something that they fear. They do not yet know that the Great Spirit is one who cares for them. Many people picture Great Spirit as one who beats them up when they do the wrong things. That kind of a picture of the Great Spirit must be let go. Only step-by-step, through surrender, can you see that the power of the Great Spirit is not against you.

Like going to the ocean, if a three year old goes to the ocean and a big wave hits them, it is going to be hard for them to believe that ocean is not against them. They just got in the wrong place at the wrong time, and that is a little bit how the Great Spirit is. It is a mighty force that has to be approached in a certain way, but not because it has a big ego and it says, "Approach me in a certain way." That would be like saying the sun has a big ego. The sun is just the sun, but it has intimacy problems because no one can get near it.

The Creator is like that because It needs to be approached in a certain way. So the Great Spirit says, "Get prepared for me. Approach me in this way so that I can give you what I want to give you." Part of the divestiture is about being in the position to receive from the power of the Great Spirit so that it can flow unobstructed into your being all the time. Otherwise, you will have obstacles that the Great Spirit tends to burn up and you will get burned up with them.

– Sun Bear

TEACHERS OF GOD

The teachers of God have a journey unto themselves. Part of that journey includes having everything of their world removed. Many who are in such a position feel that this is too rigorous and yet there is a purpose in it. There is a need to absolutely depend upon the Creator in all things as a resource, realizing humbly that everything comes from the Source. It is only in this way true security. Fulfillment and learning can take place for a teacher of God. All other possibilities, all other realities do not offer as much opportunity for true revelation and awakening. This is just one stage and it is not forever. The steps that follow are not permanent either, but are parts of shifting into the truth of the light.

Those who are the teachers of God can be recognized for they have one thing, perhaps above all other things, and that is trust. They trust that the world works, that the universe works. This trust is frequently tested, as is their faith. It is perhaps better to say that your faith and trust are indeed forged, created by the experiences you have as the teacher of God. The faith that is developed is a faith that says that the Source of this existence can truly heal, awaken and give support. The trust that is developed comes expressly and singularly from this period that can only be called 'undoing'. While this need not be painful, it is usually experienced as painful by those going through it.

During this time of undoing the only vision that exists of the future exists as a sense of things, with nothing being concrete. The plan to be revealed, exists as a call to your destiny and that destiny may never turn out to be exactly the way any part of the picture appears at any time prior to that. Yet that which is the destiny does come about in such a way as is greater than the picture the teacher of God senses. It can only be recognized in clear and essential understanding through acceptance, especially when your painful feelings are present.

– Miriam

TELEPATHY

Two of the sixty-four gifts of ascension are empathy and telepathy, which are extensions of each other. One who is telepathic is usually also empathic. The telepath becomes so aware of the needs of other people that they eventually literally perceive the needs of the other as words in their own consciousness. That is a telepathic message.

There are two types of telepathic expression, which are sending and receiving. Some people are better at getting their message across while others are better at receiving messages. The sender telepathy people are usually very good at being in charge of situations. If someone is not a good sender, they can talk as much as they want and nobody listens. But, a good sender can say anything and everyone gets it.

A good receiver is usually someone who likes other peoples' business. If you are a gossip, you are probably also a good receiving telepath.

– *Dormor*

THINGS

There are those of you who say that you have meditated and had different practices, but if only you could hear more clearly and more directly from you inner guidance it would be so much easier. I wonder what it is you are asking about. I wonder if you are saying, "Should it be this job or that job? Spirit, tell me. Should it be this place or that place? Spirit, tell me. Should it be this soul mate or that soul mate? Spirit, tell me. Should it be the green car or the red car? Should it be this food program or that food program? What is the best method for me to lose weight?"

We do not have bodies. We do not know which method you should use to lose weight. When you die you will lose all the weight that you will ever have. We do not know about driving cars and cannot tell you about cars. In fact, most of the jobs you have are nothing like anything we have had, so we cannot tell you which job is better. Most of us who are remembered by you in this world, who are now in Spirit, have not even had relationships of the kind you have, so we cannot even tell you who your soul mates are.

Now, that is not true of all of us. Some of us who help you have lived in recent enough eras to have your kind of jobs, cars, soul mates and things of this nature. Yet, have you ever wondered why people die? Maybe it is because the time has come to be finished with those things for a while. Maybe those things do not hold all the clues that you are seeking.

The best you can do with all of those things is live righteously so that they do not get in your way. You have to find out what is right for you and live that way. However, there is something that gets in the way of doing that. It is a part of your nature that you must seek and cultivate in order for it to carry you. If you do not cultivate this part of your nature, you will be left to your instinctual nature, which easily gets out of balance.

Now, nothing is wrong with your instinctual nature. Your instinctual nature is beautiful, although oftentimes confused. You tend to think you would be happy if only you could balance all of your needs, which are really the needs of your instincts. The fulfillment of your instinctual nature is confused with the experience of Nirvana, enlightenment and God consciousness. "If only I could have some physical security, emotional security, social acceptance or sexual gratification, then it would be all right." But, have you ever noticed this is like spinning plates on sticks? When you spin one plate, the other plate stops. And what if you get all of the plates spinning all at once? You will find you have to keep spinning them all or they will all stop.

You can have the things that your instinctual nature demands if you are willing to pay the price, which is their maintenance. You see, this is what we find also, "Oh please God, bring me a soul mate. Oh please God, make this soul mate the way I want him to be. Oh please God, they will not be the way I want them to be. Get them out of my life." There is a cost for those things and if you want them, you must be willing to maintain those things. That is the price.

–Shakyamuni Siddhartha Gautama (the Buddha)

TIME

The belief in time comes from the sense of a struggle and that there is a limited time. "I am going to die. I must fight before it is too late." When you are out of the struggle, the need to perceive time in the way that limits you begins to disappear and time means less. Instead of time being the issue, the issue becomes right timing. Right timing starts to become an automatic principle by which you function.

You have experienced this synchronicity. You can be at the right place at the right time or at the wrong place at the wrong time, which is equally synchronous to the negative. You have a longing for that synchronicity and become very angry and frustrated when you are not in it. That is a part of your ascension desire.

– Merlin

❖❖❖

About the concept of time, it is not really about time. When you are with Me, you are with Me and that is it. There will be lots of moments like that and everything in between does not exist. When that is true, it will not be all of the time or some of the time or any time, it will just be.

The time issue creates a lot of pain and that hurts, so you want the hurt to be over. You look for the best thing you can find and try to be there constantly so that the hurt can be over. Right? That is approaching it from your hurt, which apparently is very deep and goes on and on and on.

The only way to approach it is from love. Your hurt may create desperation that may inspire you in some ways, but you will need to give it up. The approach will then be from love. Gradually you remember love more than you remember hurt and the love will heal your hurt.

Your desperation creates an aspiration that gets you to climb out of the places that you got into. Sometimes you need that, but the aspiration will also get in the way. Just love. Love me. Love anything. Love more. That love is what heals the hurt, the separation and the time issue.

– God

❖❖❖

I think of time as permanent or eternal. In other words, it does not matter if time is short or long. I am interested in right timing, which is God's time. In God's time, its length is irrelevant. Whatever it is that is needed now, you flow with, which is what eternal is.

Ask each day to be guided in alignment for whatever is your right path for that day. You cannot make a future plan with a preset outcome because that kind of control keeps you from a daily surrender. You must be flexible and let go of outcomes. Everybody has hard places where they need to let go.

– Sun Bear

TRANSFORMATION/TRANSMUTATION

In the center of your being is also the Center of Being Itself. As you embrace this sacred center, you are transformed and transmuted from the inside out, undergoing what might be termed an inside job.

Confrontation of your personal will is typical of those of you who embrace the light because your will is met by the will of the Most High. What is now your individual will may, at one time, have been the will of the Creator. What you now utilize to hold dearly to grip the light may be that which you must let go because it has become too identified with what you think is you, when in fact the Creator pleads with you to move on further to a new and unfolding identity.

It is important to remain humble and teachable. Remember that you are always guided, protected and given assistance from the Supreme. No matter what appears to be on the outside, it is only important that you remember to keep moving forward and asking for help. Let go of all that stands in the way of doing the bidding of the Most High, which is who you truly are.

From time to time you will be surprised that you still must ask for that which stands in the way to be removed as it keeps surfacing from day to day. Only you will be able to identify what is standing in the way, for it could sprout up like a weed in a garden in which you did not expect to find a weed. No one else will be able to determine what that weed is for you. No one else must look to you and say, "These are your weeds and you must pluck them." All must mind their own business and look to their own garden.

You will recognize for yourself your weeds that stand between you and the embrace of serenity, confidence, safety in God and in the world, experience of love, divinity and sharing. As you recognize these things, they must be offered up in helpless surrender. As they are offered up, gifts will come back immediately. First peace will come, then little by little you will see the arranging and rearranging of what had been your life as it increasingly becomes the work of God.
As the things that stand in the way are taken from you, you will be surprised to find that some things that are taken are gifts. As these gifts are given and exchanged for yet new ones, you will discover the meaning of flow and order.

The meaning of the light of God, which is your source shall be shown to you each day. You will need to be reminded of this regularly. For a time these reminders will be provided for you from many sources, but mastery must and will eventually come from within you. This is what it means to remember the sacred name of God.

There are other gifts that are given to get you through, like bridges for you to cross from one point to another. There is also the gift that is eternal, which is not only given, but must be claimed. The claiming of this gift is not once and for all, for it is claimed again and again, like the remembrance of the name of God, until you, the giver, the gift and the gift giving and receiving are all one and the same. Then life becomes an experience of receiving life in serenity on life's terms.

– *Philos*

❖❖❖

You come into the world to learn how to die graciously without fear. The death or change causes the transmutation in you, which is the only way to recognize the fact that you are infinite. If you reach some point that you feel you are complete, then you have just determined you are a finite being. But, if you are able to transmute continually, presumably with some grace, then you have defined that you are an infinite being because you can go on transitioning as much as you need. Part of the reason for coming to the earth plane is to learn how to transition. If you miss the point, there is a physical death that will help you get the point.

– *Philos*

TRUST

Trust does not come from belief, but from experience.

– *Chief Great White Eagle and Sun Bear*

❖❖❖

Trust does not come out of the blue or from teachings that make sense to you. Trust comes from receiving a certain kind of experience that is born from coming in touch with a previously untapped inner place that is deep within you, which is where the Great Spirit dwells. From contact with that place, and an openness to understanding the external world around you in relation to that place deep down within, relief appears.

It is at first a small relief and experienced only in a few places. Then these places are, in a sense, tested or expanded. In other words, you go deeper into where you are more fearful and insecure and call upon that inner resource that was previously untapped to that level. You find a connection there and begin to allow the events of the external world to be met by that inner place. It is then that event by event, person by person and circumstance by circumstance you develop a working trust and faith from which serenity comes.

– *Chief Great White Eagle, Sun Bear and Yeshua*

❖❖❖

Trust is a state of being in which fear is surrendered. In trust or faith there is great knowing that goes far beyond comprehension and understanding. Trust is the state of letting go of fear and of being at peace with life itself, with your actual and true condition. In this state of knowing, a higher dimension appears. You are a part of that higher dimension.

– *Yeshua*

❖❖❖

Nobody ever gets it just right and has perfect trust. Trust and humility do not have to be perfect trust and perfect humility. In fact, they cannot be. Fear comes from not being in control enough, which you would be if you were perfect. The fact that you shall not have perfection is because you are not in control and that is how the trust gets built. Trust is created from the spiritual experiences you have, but since life cannot be perfect there shall always be some room for fear and therefore, room for learning. It is impossible to fail this.

– *Miriam and Astarte*

❖❖❖

Trust does not necessarily mean the absence of pain or even the absence of suffering. The exercise of your trust or faith can actually lead to the surfacing of more pain or suffering. The pain and suffering surface in the presence of your greater trust, for it to move and for your psyche to embrace a sacred union.

– *Isis and Miriam*

TRUTH

You are truth. Truth is what exists eternally.

– Motambi Motombi (Mo)

❖❖❖

Reality is not the point. The point is truth. Perhaps this seems like semantics, but what I mean is that truth is a living spirit, a life force that is intelligent, unlimited and capable of change.

– Philos

❖❖❖

You are trying to learn what truth is, but you have a belief that truth is a static, unmoving reality when truth is actually an evolving state.

– Sun Bear, Chief, Tall Trees, Two Trees, Sky Walker, Sam Strong Body, Red Sky and many others

❖❖❖

Trying to measure one truth against another and seeing which is more true can only lead to disappointment because truth does not exist in philosophy, teachings nor in what I say. Truth is a living vibration.

– Motambi Motombi (Mo)

❖❖❖

Maybe what you have been taught to believe is different from the truth. If you are saying, "Why did I have to go through having been taught that," I am sorry. I have an answer for you, but you may not like it because many people do not like my answers. You will understand later. That is my answer, and I am sorry.

– God

❖❖❖

When you understand truth, it is not a sentence, a philosophy or a teaching, it is a living thing in action.

– Enoch, Philos, Isis, Rapheal and Michael

TURNING IT OVER

In your desire to surrender completely, God will expose to you all of your remaining wounded places. Some of these dark corners are so ancient that you will just need to accept the feelings as they arise. The only things to do are: 1) recognize that you are having those feelings; 2) ask for them to be lifted; 3) bless the object, person or circumstance; and 4) then turn your thoughts to helping another. If you do not do these steps, it turns into incredible self-centered anxieties that result in inner or outer dramas, which is why it must be turned over.

This is a cleansing at a level that is so beyond you that you never know what is being taken. You cannot heal these areas yourself because you have not created these as wounds in yourself. Some of this in fact, is just none of your business. Some things will be enormously humbling and some things that you think should be gone will linger. Great Spirit will always leave just a few really embarrassing traits in your being that you will never get rid of for the purpose of keeping you from being able to dissociate from your brothers and sisters. You have to own these over and over and over.

Others will say, "You mean, I do not need to be perfect to be enlightened?" Their freedom at seeing you will free you again and again. You will see yourself making it easy for others and taking the strain out of their enlightenment by being a living example of light with a few things that the Great Spirit left sprinkled that will never go away totally. These things will never distract you if you keep even reasonably spiritually fit. You do not have to create great karmas ever again and you will always be a source of great light and inspiration for yourself and others.

While your growth will go on forever, you will no longer struggle with your ego. Any time you notice a struggle, the same four things apply: acknowledge the feeling, call upon the Infinite to lift it, bless the object and give your love to somebody who needs it. You will then whisk right through all of the dramas, unless the Great Spirit wants you to learn something from them.

– Sun Bear

UNCONDITIONAL LOVE

With unconditional love you must take a mighty step, which is to let it go and let it come back in whatever form it comes back. That is hard because it means giving up control, but it is rewarding because you can have what you really want in love.

– Sun Bear, Chief, Tall Trees, Two Trees, Sky Walker, Sam Strong Body, Red Sky and many others

❖❖❖

It is not meant that you are here to get bogged down in a struggle. Nor are you because you are ignorant, or that this plane is a plane for lesser beings to live. This plane has all levels of beings living in it, from the lesser knowing to the greater knowing. There are many levels of beings in each and every plane or realm of existence.

The purpose then is not to come into this existence and figure out how to get out of it. Rather, you come into this existence to gain benefit by being here. You are here to gain joy, wisdom, light and love. It is not necessary to invalidate this plane or yourself as less worthy or that somehow you were not bright enough to exist in a dimension beyond this one.

As collectives of particles of consciousness yourselves, you too can have access to the so-called higher dimensions as well as to these more dense dimensions while you are here in the physical human body. In order to access these higher dimensions, you must be willing to learn lessons of unconditional love for yourself and others. That is the only key to the higher dimensions.

For those unwilling to embrace the lessons related to unconditional love, no access can be maintained in the higher dimensions. You may touch those higher dimensions in a number of ways and experience intoxicating levels of joy and peace. You may enter into the heavenly realms and the worlds of light or experience great and powerfully miraculous levels of existence, all while here in this world. But, only those entities amongst you willing to embrace unconditional love may remain in such an experience as that.

– *Philos*

UNIVERSE

Your universe had a definite beginning less than twenty billion years ago. Universes are creations or events that have always been going on and always will go on. There was not a time when universes began. To make it even more complicated, universes do not only happen on a kind of lateral plane. For example, the stars that you see in your sky are gleams of light or energy centers, much like the neutron of an atom. These energy centers compose your stars, your entire universe and all the clusters of universes that are separated by voids so vast as to seem infinite. Your universe is but a speck in the corporate body of a larger universe, which also has its version of stars. Each universe is a speck on an object in a larger universe still and it goes on larger and larger without end, infinitely.

It is the same with what is going on in the smaller level in the very fabric of your universe, even in your physical body. There are countless numbers of universes teaming with life forms. Somewhere, even on your fingertip, I am certain you would be able to find some universe teaming with life forms. These life forms would also be composed of smaller particles, and so it goes, worlds within worlds within worlds.

– *Miriam*

UNTAPPED POWER

Within each person is an untapped, immaculate and indescribable power that is the guiding intelligence at work throughout all of existence. This power is untapped until the time that you are entirely embraced by it because of your surrender. This force is so beautiful and so powerful that merely by its residence within your being you are benefitted by its presence. It intertwines itself eventually in some ways and at all times in all of your affairs.

There comes a point in your existence when you become aware of the untapped inner resource. It is then that your search begins to tap this Source. As you embarked upon this journey, there comes a powerful unfolding that time and time again reveals beauty, even when you live in the outer perimeter of Its beingness.

This Source requires everything to truly be known and it is the greatest teacher. There are those who have walked this journey and understand this. For those who have surrendered, whether they are great or small in stature, they are free and joyous. All that is worrisome in them is abandoned utterly, for it is tapped at that point.

Throughout this world there are many souls who have let go entirely into the truth of the recognition of this inner resource. They are not always visible, and many may not be doing what is considered outwardly great or profound, yet others are.

– *Yeshua*

VALUE

The value of your life is greater than everything else. It may not feel that way to you, so that is where your focus has to go to. Once you appreciate the value of your life you have serenity and things can go up or down, begin and end because that is the way of the world. As long as you have you, your existence and life, you have the most important things.

Pain comes when your energy and beliefs are invested in what happens to you more than in the truth of your existence. Your life force is what is important. And yes, those other things are also, but your life force does not exist to make your blood pressure go up, to make your life work or to give you a mate. That is not the purpose of your life force.

There is a lot of false collective consciousness energy going into things that do not matter and it is sweeping the intention of good people into thinking those things matter. There are not enough messages out there saying, "Listen, that does not matter as much as you. You are what matters."

– Chief Great White Eagle, Sun Bear and Miriam

VALUES

Moral values, even higher moral values, tend to be current to the time, day and understanding of a particular culture. Their source is Spirit, but it is not Spirit. These values are whatever the highest thing is upon which the collective consciousness can rely.

– Devorah

VISION

Your dreams always seem somehow within reach or just out of reach if only for more patience, determination, education, development or awakening of some kind. A vision is that of which you are possessed and remains with you throughout life. A vision seems incomprehensible and not achievable, and is such an inward demand that you may even feel at times as much tortured by it as blessed by it.

– Miriam, Isis and QuanYin

WILL

The highest intention is a will, which you are a part of, that is greater than your own will. It is a will that is an empowered version of who you are that you do not yet know yourself to be. It is a will that gives you the opportunity to expand and become harmonious with It so that any union of light is without a tremor and is experienced as a journey of great joy.

– Philos

WILLINGNESS

You do not have to be able to do something, just willing. Willingness is everything. Once there is willingness, there is no stopping the Spirit from coming in. Everything can then happen.

– Sun Bear, Chief Great White Eagle and Great Bear

❖❖❖

Continue to seek light through your spiritual experiences, for they shall lead you to an awakening. Never put aside that search, no matter how seemingly impractical or how sincere you believe you are. While your sincerity matters, it will come if you are simply willing. But, if you do not have it initially, it does not matter if you are simply willing. The sincerity will come with your honesty because you have been willing. Your openness will follow and then instruction from the Divine Itself will embrace you every step of the way, asking you for only one thing, which is surrender.

– Dormor

WISHES

What Spirit wishes, does not matter. What matters is that you come to understand what you want. What you want is what Spirit wishes. The only reason that some of you might feel that this is not true is because you have a judgment about yourself as wrong or that something you want must be somehow befouled. It is not true, but that is why it is important to do so much work on yourself. The work is not because you need fixing, but because you need a lot of time spent discovering and knowing yourself. It is not that anything is broken, but there is something that is unknown and unfamiliar. You must know it, learn it, see it and experience it because it is a great deal less concrete than a lot of other things. Nevertheless, concrete is not the criterion for powerful experience.

– Sun Bear

WORTHINESS

One great misnomer of the people in your era, a very fundamentally flawed idea that is accepted culturally, is this idea of worthiness. If a person does not feel worthy, the culture says that they must come to terms with their worthiness by simply accepting it, finding a beautiful part within their spirit that shows them they are worthy and deeply accepting it. This idea is a false truth. In reality, not only must you find it, but then you must prove it. You cannot feel worthy until you do something that makes you worthy, otherwise you will always doubt your worthiness.

– Great Bear, Sun Bear, Amatunkwa, Philos, Enoch and Merlin

❖❖❖

I understand that you do not feel good enough and that is why you think you have to be someone else or need this or should do that. I cannot help myself when it comes to you; I love you completely, always and forever. It is impossible for me to feel anything else for you. I love you when you are clear. I love you when you are unclear. I love you when you are doubtful. I love you when you have faith. I love you when you are high. I love you when you are silly. I love you when I give things. I love you when I take things away. I love you always and eternally without a limit, without end, beyond all your knowing. I place my love in certain ones around you who are able to love you the way that I am able to love you.

You are worthy. If you do not feel worthy, I will keep sending you angels, teachers and signs. Those things are wonderful and I will send them if you want, but it is tiresome for me to wait for you. I ache to have you with me completely. Just believe me and claim that you are worthy. Your disbelief will surface, but decide it is worth more to you to believe me than not to believe me.

I do not want you to believe in me. I want you to know me. Believe that you are worthy and that will teach you to know me. Only through your belief in your worthiness can you then know me. Your belief in your unworthiness will prevent you from knowing me. Do you need help with this? I want to give you help. The help is yours right now.

– God

❖❖❖

In this modern day there is a principle that is often proffered and I cannot stand it. That is this idea of loving yourself and the way that it is offered. The reason I cannot stand it is because it is a suggestion that a person finds self-esteem from affirming they are worthy when they have not proven their own worthiness to themselves or to others. You cannot feel worthy about yourself until you consistently do something worthy. If you have not done something that makes you feel worthy, then you cannot feel worthy. You must do hard work about something in order to feel worthy of it.

-- Merlin, Chief Great While Eagle, Amatunkwa and Enoch

WOUNDS

Sometimes you may have an investment in seeing something in a particular way, which is based on a compensation for an inner wound. You may have that set up as your highest goal because it may feel like the most urgent or pressing matter to you. However, that may not be the next step for you. Your spirit may be trying to give you messages that may not even feel significant or relevant because of those inner wounds and the orientation to having those wounds addressed in the way you want them addressed.

You must give up certain investment in what you have set up for yourself and be willing to see what the universe has in store for you. Many people confuse that with giving up their will. From my perspective it is the discovery of your own true will. You give up being without a true will because you have no true choice if you are compelled by a wound that you have no control over. When you are addicted to a particular need you cannot see clearly.

– Philos

❖❖❖

The Great Spirit loves to be beckoned, especially when it comes to a shift in a wound in your own nature. Great Spirit addresses that wound immediately. Great Spirit does not always immediately address the outside affairs of your life. When the issue is located on the inside and addressed, then Great Spirit does the inside job and the outside job seems to happen in short order.

– Sun Bear, Chief, Tall Trees, Two Trees, Sky Walker, Sam Strong Body, Red Sky and many others

❖❖❖

There are always certain issues in your life that are extensions into the physical plane of your wounds. Those things are normal and will always continue throughout your life as a means to help you be honest with yourself. There is no need to seek perfection in the sense that your external life should always be without quirks or little surprises. When there are increasing acceptance and surrender in your heart toward the Spirit of the Universe, you feel empowerment, enlightenment, love and gentleness, which increasingly spreads through all of your affairs.

– Chief Great White Eagle, Sun Bear, Yeshua, Olga, Helga, and Devorah

YOU

You are my devotion, my heart, the reason that I exist. You are everything to me. There is nothing that means more to me than you. I exist because of you, for you and through you and there is nothing else.

– God

❖❖❖

What you need to do is be who you are no matter what. Even when you do everything right and things still happen to go wrong, be who you are. The passing of the test is an experience within you in which the outer world simply does not matter as much to you anymore. It cannot hurt you and you do not fear it.

This state of being is an arrival, an initiation, an accomplishment, which does not come from simply working at it or aspiring to it. It is an achievement in that it is a matter of you holding your center sometimes simply because you believe it will work, but ultimately because you see that is what matters.

In the holding of your center, where you keep loving and receiving love, Spirit and you, who are one, sends things to your aid that support you. At the point when holding your center is the only thing you are about, not because you have pushed other things out of your mind, but because you have become so true to who you really are and what you are really here to do, then nothing else matters to you. The fear that can now sometimes come on strong, then holds no power over you anymore. Your fear then turns into excitement.

– *Philos*

❖❖❖

Who you are is an experience, is it not? And that experience of who you are is, in a sense like a revelation, a discovery, a surprise that goes on within your awareness and your being. That revelation is who you are and who you are becoming. Events happen so that you can discover more about you.

– *Philos*

YOUR NATURE

Those of you, who have had a little bit of awakening, need to share that awakening by giving it away. That is how it works. Most importantly though, you must be willing to look at yourselves and clear your karmas.

Your natures will drive you crazy sometimes. Your sexual nature will become entirely lustful. I know this is not popular and it will make you crazy because you will not be able to figure out so many things. Your physical desire for security will make you feel like you cannot stop, you just cannot get enough, you want more and more and more. Also your desire to be accepted will cause you to either try to please everybody or control everybody.

Sometimes you must beg the Creator to save you from these things. Do not worry because you will be able to have plenty of sex. It is all right to do that. And you do not have to give up all of your money or your work. You do not have to walk with your face toward the ground saying, "Yes, I am one humble, two humble, three humble." You do not have to do any of that.

You will just turn out to be exactly like you are, but you will shine more. You will not be fighting with the others who are fighting for the same things for which you are fighting. You will not be clashing wills everywhere. You can get about the business for which you have come here into this world. The voice of Spirit will speak very strongly to you and you will be able to hear it.

– *Shakyamuni Siddhartha Gautama (the Buddha)*

ANNEX

THE BUDDHA

The Buddha was in great pain from endless work on himself. He went from Master to Master to Master perfecting different techniques of self-realization, but he did not feel any better. All of the other Masters' disciples who watched how perfectly the Buddha practiced these techniques became very impressed with him. They would ask him what was special about him and he would call them fools saying, "Do you not see, none of this works? I practiced all of these techniques and I am still miserable." They could not comprehend what he was saying.

The Buddha was so distressed, disappointed and hateful toward the Creator for torturing him with no peace, even though he did all the things that these Masters would say, he finally decided he was going to die. He would merge into the light and in essence, have a talk with God about His system. By that time though, he had come to believe that it was wrong to kill anything including himself, so he had a dilemma. He decided that he was simply not going to take any food or water and just meditate until death. But, he had become such a yogi with his practices that he did not die when he meditated. In an extraordinary dilemma, he meditated and meditated and would not move.

Finally the Buddha attained enlightenment. He had a great realization that his problem was guilt. He thought that he was being made to suffer because something was incredibly wrong with him. He also thought that the whole world was being made to suffer because something was incredibly wrong with them. His years spent studying with the different Masters and Yogis, trying to purge himself or purify himself from what was wrong, were causing him greater and greater pain. When he meditated, he realized his beauty and that beauty made him realize, "I was mistaken. I am not horrible, but I am beautiful." He conceded this realization down deep in his heart.

Most people who realize this do not have it all at once. It is like an awakening that occurs and it may occur through several events and circumstances throughout their life. Some may never realize it deeply enough, but it is the same sort of awakening to a lesser degree.

The Buddha went to find all of the people who had wanted to follow him before. Many of them were monks that he had shunned and turned away. Finding them he said, "I understand now! I understand! It is nothing. You do not have to do anything! You are beautiful! I am beautiful!" They said, "Well, maybe you are beautiful. You have always been special. But tell us, what did you really do Bodhisattva?"

He could not get them to believe that they did not have to do anything. So he said, "Maybe if I get them to do what I did, they will have the same revelation I had." He essentially tortured them with disciplines. Some of them did realize their beauty, but they could not achieve any of the disciplines. When they did achieve some, he would give them more and make the disciplines harder until eventually they would give up and surrender. That was the Buddha's way of teaching.

– Miriam

CHIEF GREAT WHITE EAGLE

When I was John the Beloved, I died a few years after Yeshua left. I was crucified, put to death and born again amongst the Native people where I became Chief many years later. When I was nineteen, Yeshua came. At first he did not recognize me, but my heart recognized him. Then one day, after spending a year and a half with my people, he turned to me and said, "Yes, John, I remember you," like he had always known. I think it was as much a surprise to him as it was to me. I do not think he did know, but it just came to him. He was much older and in a different wavelength by then.

I did not know how it would happen, but one day I was called to do a great work. I was to teach some of the ways to other people. It caught on, becoming a huge teaching that spread across the land to many peoples and many shamans. I could not sit at the head of this, but in my lifetime it grew and evolved into the Sun Bear tradition. At that time, little organizations, each with their own leadership, sprouted up to train shamans.

I had given so much to this work that I was sick and unhealthy. My wife and I were very, very poor and had nothing. By this time Yeshua was long gone. Many had picked up my work after me and were prospering in the same work I was doing. I, who had given my life, had nothing.

One day a Chief pulled me aside and said, "White Eagle, why are you not taking the gifts that people are giving you. You are sick and sometimes we think you are dying. You never have anything. You need to be charging for your work." I did not want to do that. He talked to me for a while and I said, "You known, you are right. I know I need to do something like that."

One day I was in a meditation during a vision quest and I thought I heard the voice of God telling me that this Chief was right. I needed to receive something now so that I could be comfortable. I was still fairly young at the time, but I was not healthy.

One day, when I was in my early thirties, I went to the people who were closest to me when I first started my work. When I met with these people, who were big honchos by this time, I told them that maybe we should start charging for our work. They had been receiving gifts and some had more than others. They looked at each other and at me and said, "You cannot do that White Eagle. There are many who have access to the teachings now. If they follow this route and money is required, they could not do it."

I heard them, and in this instance they were right. What happened was the Spirit of God no longer spoke to me only through me. It spoke through a group conscience that reflected the Great Spirit's will because the Great Spirit's will had been instituted, spoken and laid out. The work had created access to awakening and healing throughout many nations. It was no longer my work and was out of my hands. I realized I was fine with this and I would receive gifts from those who wanted to give, but that I would not charge.

– *Chief Great White Eagle*

GOD

I am a herald. The Source sends me, and those like me for the purpose of helping people to get ready to know God. I am a manifestation of the Source. We all are manifestations of the Source, but you define yourself in certain ways that give you a separate picture of you and of Source. What is this idea of having a God outside of you? God is both outside and within.

I cannot tell you what God is because it is an experience and you can only know God by being in love with It. I can tell you this, God is that which inspires a devotional ecstasy in people, which is decidedly personal rather than impersonal. There really is no way to describe God. It is all of the things you could describe, but there is an experience that takes place that gets stronger and stronger.

Some people think of God as an energy field that is the most intelligent being in the universe, but that is another being. It is better to refer to God when you talk about love.

There is God and there is also light. Lord is the form God takes that you are more easily able to access in a personal way. The Spirit Guides can also be a form of God, but you see, Lord and God are the same things. Sometimes God takes a form that people do not feel is so impersonal and that is the principle that people usually call Lord of the Universe, which means that is your personalized God. God can also be 'Source' or 'My Beloved.'

Then there is the Monad, which means the All Thing, or the All That Is. Within the Monad moves a force called God, which moves the All Thing to evolve. So you could say God is the energy within the Monad, the One Thing, the All Thing, the Ultimate Intelligence. The Monad is all intelligence, all awareness, even bad awareness, even things that are not useful and even negative things. God includes the negative, but no bad because God, the Source, is not a container.

The Source is called Source because it is what serves to move the Monad. Before that, the Monad was just eternity, just existence that existed as nothing but virtual particles, virtual energy, then the Source moved it.

The Source is an energy that has a distinct personality for individual entities. Whether you need it or not, entities that are aspects of the Creator meet and experience a Creator with a personality. That personality, whatever it might be for that entity, would be different with a different entity. That is not because they need it, but because the Creator is like a lover. That is romantic you see, and do you not see how the universe is one big romance? God is an incredible artist with a temperament and with motivations. That is very different from what you might conceptualize, but the Creator, the Source definitely has its own distinct flair and flavor.

What you need is to develop your own personal relationship with God. That means you should acknowledge or recognize this power demonstrating in your consciousness and in your life more and more. Every time you feel that power, acknowledge it and say thank you. That is one of the things you must know about Source, God is a sucker for love. Any time you have great appreciation for Source, It just wants to give more and more to you.

– Constance

MIRIAM

I was the only daughter and only child of my parents, born to them late in their lives. My father was a very noted Rabbi so when he had no children, this was not seen as good. When my mother became pregnant and was to give birth to me, this was considered impossible for it was thought she was too old.

Upon my birth, my father was most excited as well as my mother. In those times, if you were an only child and a girl this was not seen as good for there would be no one to carry on the name. Nevertheless my father, otherwise a strict traditionalist, became extremely enamored with me and taught me all of the ancient teachings as well as the Hebrew teachings. I had a thirst for these things.

Before I was fourteen, I married a man of almost forty. In that day that was very, very old, but it was common for men to marry much younger women. For my years and for my time I was considered very, very bright by modern standards. Today I believe intelligence is measured, unfortunately, by a formula of factors called the Intelligence Quotient. Perhaps mine would have been an IQ beyond 185. I was very bright, but very innocent.

One day, after my marriage, an Angel appeared to me and told me that I was to bear a child who would be called the Son of Man. This was not the only apparition, for I was given to many such prophecies. Several months later, an Angel again appeared and said, "I am the Angel of the Lord! I bear the seed of the child to whom you shall give birth." I believed it was the Angel of the Lord. There is much more to the story, this being but a brief part.

Yusef, my husband, had four daughters previous to our marriage, all of them older than I. They did not take well to this story and neither did Yusef. He was too old and wise to believe that it was an Angel who impregnated me, but I was intelligent enough to hold to my story for I knew he would not believe as I would believe.

Yusef, to tell you the truth, never believed me fully. But he loved me a great deal and accepted it in time. Yeshua, whom most now mistakenly call Jesus, was the first of my many children and was very different and very special. All of my children were special, but they were never in tune with Yeshua. All of them viewed Yeshua as a little bit 'daft' but loved him dearly, much in the same way that you might love your brother if you did not think he had all of his wits about him. Because he was also brilliant, he had a way of penetrating all confusion from a very early age. He saw things in a simple, simple way. His brothers and sisters loved him, but they also saw him as so different that they did not understand him fully.

I was his first teacher and taught him well. I helped awaken his interests in things spiritual and metaphysical, as he had a great, great thirst. Many teachers did visit him, but not on the night of his birth. For years we were discovered in one place after another, and we were brought many teachers from different parts of the world. I learned how to interpret the teachings for Yeshua. So thirsty was he that before age fifteen he left to search out the brilliance of the knowledge that had been brought to him in his youth. He left for years.

James, the next youngest brother, was his only brother who did not really like Yeshua. He resented Yeshua for having interests that took him away from his responsibility as the eldest boy and left the care of the family for James. Yusef died and left the youngest to take care of things. He was the next oldest boy after James and was the only one who did not consider Yeshua to be crazy, but thought him to be shrewd and somewhat diabolical or egotistical. Even though this was an unfortunate rift between two brothers, this rift healed in another life. There is much more to that story, but enough for now.

Yeshua has not incarnated in a body since that time, but has come and visited through many oracles and mediums throughout history. He shall not come again to this earth in a body, but his spirit comes now. It is the spirit of awakened consciousness that causes so many to be closer to their inner, divine nature. The time he spoke of returning has already come, but it was not in a physical body.

Yeshua became one in a state of ascendancy where many have become one. Anyone who becomes one in that ascended nature does not only become one with Yeshua, but with all who have ascended. That spirit into which human beings ascend represents the highest available experience for human beings. It is not the highest experience in all the universe, just the fullest potential of humans. Occasionally, an aspect of that collective ascended awareness manifests itself in the form of one person or another, giving that person an opportunity to express itself as a fully ascended being, and to be recognized as an Avatar, a Christed entity.

When Yeshua spoke of his returning that was quite a different matter than people of this day see it. Yeshua was sincere, powerful and enlightened, yet made many errors. When he returned from his journeys to Persia, India, Afghanistan and many other lands, there were few who could understand him. There were few that he could relate to on a level that they could appreciate, for they lacked his experience and breadth of travel. So, he spoke in a very simplistic way to a people who were largely uneducated.

The various clergy were so full of their own beliefs that he had to speak to the ordinary people if he wanted to receive any openness. Although much of what is in your Bible is changed and not true, there are some things that Yeshua did say that have been the source of much controversy and difficulty. Yeshua was filled only with love, and yet he felt his own power. He felt it was his duty to save our people, and he felt he had to get their attention. It was a mistake for him to be understood as THE Son of God, for he spoke of all as sons and daughters of God. His true mission was to introduce a new idea, the idea of a God who was compassionate and loving. Until that day all the gods of the day were seen as vengeful things to be feared and who required great sacrifice. People gave the best parts of their crops and animals in a day where there was already so much poverty, ignorance and suffering that only a few survived beyond suffering.

After thousands of years of relating to a vengeful and vindictive God, who could hear of a God of love? Who would believe him? No one would believe him. So, in order to get their attention he said, "If there is a God who demands a sacrifice, then I am God's son and I shall be the final sacrifice." He said this in the way that perhaps could end their concept of a God that is vindictive and relate to what he was speaking about as a God of love. If you give it any thought however, how could a God be a God that demands blood in order for fair treatment? That comes out of the mind of humankind and not out of the heart of God.

Yeshua went along with that to get their attention, but he became driven into thinking that it was his duty to get the people's attention and force them to listen for their own sake. That was a terrible error, for what it has created for generations hence is more people thinking of suffering and sacrifice in order to know God or love. What it has created are people who are ready to kill in God's name and people who are ready to force their beliefs upon others. It also led to Yeshua's own physical demise.

Yeshua did die and he did come back. This was something that he had learned to do in India, which you would call a comatose state. In this period where he ought to have been dead, he had a communion with God, whom he called the Father and the Father told him, "Go back and undo what you have done." Yeshua did not fully understand right away what that meant. However, what he tried to do was to speak to those who were closest to him, who were seventy-four in number, not twelve. He tried to get them to understand some of what he learned in his journeys so as to do things differently. His intention was not to proclaim himself as the Son of God, but as one whose words and knowledge could lead people to know the Temple or God within.

Not even his disciples understood him by this time for he had promulgated such a different way of looking at things that they could not really hear him. So, within two months he left them. He told them he would be back to help them before their last days. He did not say THE last days, but their last days. He wandered off into the land of his early learning, visiting the disciples in the way that you might call an astral sense, sending the form of his presence to each of them on a number of occasions. This is why they thought him to ascend, for they saw his being appear and disappear, like a body of light. While astrally appearing, he himself was elsewhere, which was also something he had learned to do in the Orient.

In his journeys he continued his teachings in many places around the world: Persia, India, Afghanistan, the Polynesian Islands, China and Japan. He sailed with the Polynesians clear around the world, eventually making his way to South America and to the lands that you now call Peru, Central America, Mexico and the southern regions of the United States. There he taught amongst the Indians. He married in Japan, had children and died a normal death at about age 111. His birthday was the twenty-first of March as you measure time, and he was dark skinned with dark eyes.

– *Miriam*

ST. FRANCIS (FRANCESCO)

It took me eleven thousand years from the time I met my Master Teacher Yeshua to my fulfillment. When Yeshua offered me instantaneous freedom, not only was I not ready, I could not see it. When my Master came to me, he said, "Give me everything. Give up everything here and come with me." He said that in his presence I would be free, but until I experienced my actual bondage, I could not ask to be free of it.

I turned to the Master and said, "You do not understand me, and I misunderstood you. You are a cruel man, not a caring one." I had to turn away from the Master and go back into my life rather than into the light with him. I just was not ready and I could not complete then. It was not my time, not my season just as I could no more plant an apple seed in the winter and expect it to grow. I do not fault myself for that.

I turned away from the Master at that time and took eleven hundred years to learn to do one other thing. I thought my condition was not enough, so I sought a more and more evolved expressions of that condition. In that eleven hundred years I lived many lifetimes until I reached the pinnacle of what I thought would fulfill me. My family was very powerful and wealthy. I had a woman I was assigned to marry whom I loved. I had kindness from my family of birth, and I had my whole life laid out for me.

Finally, I recognized where I was bound. I was bound by the things that promised me freedom. I could not let go of the things that wer binding me, even though I was in pain. I loved my wife and chil and was devoted to them. I was also attached to them and to m could not find my soul's fulfillment. I thought those things wo me. I truly did. But somehow, because of my past life experie the trap and remembered that I had some form of this ove again. I felt burdened and systematically set about freeing m than achieving more.

I did have vanity when I was here on earth. That is why I shaved a spot on my head, but I was never comfortable with that. So, the way that I exist now, in this dimension, is that I wear my bald spot. This may seem like a little thing to you, but it was not to me. Now that I am on this side, whereas most entities appear in their astral form the way that they are most beautiful in the physicality, I have retained my bald spot. This is like a joke here, but this was not a joke to me while I was in the world. In fact, so much so that I insisted that everyone who followed me shave a bald spot. I forced them to do this, even though it was my issue.

– Francesco

YESHUA

Right before I was born into this world, my mother had a visitation by an angel named Gabriel. He told her that she would bear a child who would be called the Son of Man. This was indeed a fantastic surprise for her, she herself being a child of only thirteen.

As the only child of her father, a Rabbi well into his elder years, she had always been a favored child. Although she was a girl, my grandfather did school her and raise her, giving her all the privileges and advantages given to the first born son of those times. He, being a man of conservative background, gave up those former ideas for he did so love his daughter Miriam. She was a brilliant woman who by today's standards would be measured of an IQ of about 185. That is far beyond most of your day.

In my younger years, no matter where we went in our journeys, I was visited by wise ones, for it had been heralded that I would come. For years there was a bounty upon all younger males beneath a certain age. But, wherever we would go, I would be visited by those who would bring gifts of scripts and teachings that they did share with my mother and her with me. When I got to be of age, I did leave my home in search of the teachers who did come to my mother in my younger years.

I did find them and others in my journeys and when I did come of understanding, returned to the land of my youth to teach. I was filled with inspiration and desire for I felt within me a great light and a great power. I did come to believe that it was my duty, as it was my joy, to share of these things. But, in my journeys and from my studies I had come to understand that which is far, far beyond a simpler people. Because of this, it was indeed my service to be of assistance in this world.

I did think that it was important to draw great attention to myself. I ught that if I could persuade persons to regard me, then for their good they would be lifted. I did come to think this for I saw it as uty to heal this world, indeed to save this world.

Because of this intention I did create seventy-four people closest to me, not twelve as many have come to believe. I did draw to me such attention as that it did also draw enemies to me. Eventually it led to something that is to this day still misunderstood.

Indeed I was tortured and put to my death as I knew that I would be. Upon my union with the light I was called into the center and I did meet the Source of Existence there for the first time in this manner. The Source, which I called the Father, did say to me, "Yeshua, what have you done? Go back and undo what you have done." And so I did this for I had come to understand that it was not my duty to save this world, but simply to give that which I have understood.

I did not rise into the heavens, but began a journey that lasted for many, many years through the same lands where I had done my learning. This time I traveled as a teacher through the Near East and Far East, Afghanistan, India, Persia, eventually to Japan and China, back down through the southeastern part of Asia and further south still into the South Seas Islands. With the Polynesians I did sail clear to South America, for they did not look to the stars to sail the seas but to the currents of the water. They were by far the greatest sea persons of all of the known world.

Arriving in the lands now called Peru, I journeyed up through the northern parts of South America, through those lands now called Central America, Mexico and even in the southern regions of what is now called the United States. I finally settled in Japan where I took a wife, had children and lived until 111.

Everything that I have told to you has been written. In the time after my leaving of this world many did seek to take the information that was left behind by me and many of the disciples. They gathered it to them and used this for the purposes of developing control over the people. The ones who propagated the idea of Christianity were not any of the disciples whom I had known, but rather Paul of Tarsis who did come 250 years after me.

– *Yeshua*